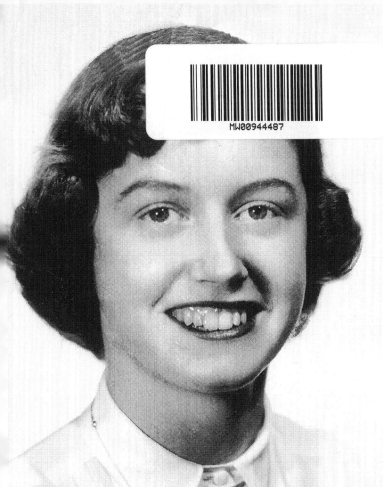

Kraminson Days

from white gloves
to black robes
and beyond

✝

A Memoir by

MARY MARGARET PHELAN WERNER,
J.S.C. RET.

ISBN: 1483922839
ISBN 13: 9781483922836

*I dedicate this book to my husband, Dr. Larry Werner,
for over 60 years of Kraminson Days.*

Kraminson Days

FROM WHITE GLOVES TO BLACK ROBES AND BEYOND

Table of Contents

About the Author

O N THE OCCASION OF MY EIGHTIETH BIRTHDAY MY CHIL-
DREN DECIDED THAT I SHOULD PUBLISH MY MEMOIRS,
WRITTEN PIECEMEAL OVER THE LAST SIX YEARS. These stories recount bits and pieces of a life, my life, which
in a very real way tracks the movement of women in
history from home and kitchen and kids to school
and second careers and beyond, a time of incredible change and challenge and rewards. It's never
been boring, at least not yet.

I am a Catholic School kid, married 57 years
to the same wonderful man, have seven children,
fifteen grandchildren and three great grandchildren. I am an attorney, a retired New York State
Supreme Court Justice, and an active participant
in OLLI, a lifelong learning program at Stony
Brook University; a member of several Bar Associations, and of the Board of The Energeia Partner-
ship and of the Board of Advisors of Erase Racism.

My mom and dad were first generation Irish
American. My mother was 'a stay at home' mom
and my father a New York City Policeman.

I was the middle child and we all were the first
in the family to attend college. My sister and I went
to St. John's University Teachers' College when it

was hardly a university, but rather a couple of old buildings located in Brooklyn, one out on Lewis and Willoughby Avenues by the Myrtle Avenue El and the other downtown.

In true Vincentian fashion, the building on Lewis Avenue was the College for men during the daytime hours, nine to three and became the Teachers' College for mostly women from four to nine and all day Saturday. There was one hour in between during which the day school men met the Teachers' College women in the cafeteria and many marriages resulted. In my husband's class alone, Mario Cuomo met Mathilda Raffa, Joe McDonald met Marie Lowell, Joe Cline met Betty Jackson and I met and fell in love with my husband, Larry Werner. We women all had part-time jobs in order to pay the tuition but were sure to be available for that witching hour.

One of my college jobs was at Old St Patrick's School on Mott Street in Manhattan where I was hired to teach 60 third graders from eight to one. The little Sister of Charity nun who hired me told me when I started that there were two rules I should follow: "Don't lose anyone and don't let them get the best of you." I didn't lose anyone and they didn't get the best of me. I cannot really vouch for what they learned, but I survived.

After three years I quit college so that we could get married. And we did in 1955, when I was twenty-one and he was a sophomore at Cornell Medical School. By the time he graduated and had finished his internship at King's County Hospital we had three babies, he was a Captain in the Air Force and we were on our way to his first assignment, the Philippine Islands, a place as far away from Brooklyn as one could go without coming back. We were married for 57 years.

Many times in later years I remembered those rules: when I was dealing with my own brood of seven children, when I taught my youngest who was born deaf to speak, when I traveled by propeller planes to the Philippine Islands with my Air Force Doctor husband, when I lived in Albany Georgia for the last year of his enlistment and saw black people treated like dirt, when I marched in Smithtown for open housing, or in Washington against the War in Vietnam, when I decided to go back to finish my education at forty and go to Law School, when I was one of only eight women out of a hundred ADA's in the Suffolk County District Attorney's Office, and the first woman Bureau Chief, when I was the first woman on the Supreme Court Bench in Suffolk County, I didn't lose anyone and I didn't let them get the best of me.

When my husband and I retired we enrolled in the Osher Life Long Learning Institute (OLLI) at Stony Brook University, he in some science and history courses, and I in the Memoir Writing Course led by two wonderful teachers:

Sheila Beiber and Dorothy Schiff-Shannon and these memoirs are the result of six years in that class.

Kraminson Days

M<small>Y TITLE?</small> Well...
I had an Aunt Kay, my mom's only sister, who was a single lady, without beaus as far as we knew. She was a gentle softie who my sister, Joan, and I loved. I'm sure my brother, Edward, loved her also, but Joan and I had her to ourselves for seven years before he was born. Aunt Kay "went to business" as we used to say and worked her way up in the Kendall Mills office in Manhattan over the course of some fifty years. I have her fifty year pin with a beautiful blue stone. Is it a real gem stone? Who knows? It doesn't matter.

Kraminson (**krǎ'** min-son) is a word that was Aunt Kay's creation. Anything that was full to overflowing, that was good, really good, almost beyond words, was Kraminson Day. Growing up we always thought it was an Irish word, but in checking with my Irish relatives, they never heard of it. And so it will remain, for now, without further research, Aunt Kay's word and as such I am sure she would be proud for me to use it to title these rambling, episodic, memories of a life that can only, so far, be described as one of many "Kraminson Days".

"White gloves"

My high school years were spent at St. Saviour's in Park Slope, Brooklyn, which required as part of the uniform, white gloves, hats and stockings. One of the only almost bawdy jokes among the girls was to wonder what if we came to school with only the hat, gloves and stockings. It was a rigorous, but unenlightened education, full of fun, field hockey in Prospect Park in our ridiculous jumpers and bloomers, and an orchestra that was most dreadful in which I, a fairly accomplished pianist, played first violin since according to Sister De La Salle if I could play the piano I certainly could play the violin.

"Black Robes"

Eventually, after seven children, I returned to college and then Law School; became an Assistant District Attorney in the Suffolk County District Attorney's Office; was appointed and then elected a Judge of the New York State Supreme Court.

"And Beyond"

And then retirement and the good fortune of finding a program at Stony Brook University, a Life Long Learning Program and a Memoir Writing class and hence after five years of writing I have this gathering of memories which my children have insisted I publish.

And so I begin.

Many of the players are already gone: my mother, my father, Aunt Kay, Uncle Bill, my sister, Joan, and most importantly my husband, Larry. We called him Big Larry. Our first son was named Lawrence after his father obviously, but because his delivery was miraculous his middle name is Jude, Patron Saint of Hopeless Cases, which makes for lots of confusion since my husband was Lawrence Joseph. So our son was to be distinguished from his father as Little Larry and his father as Big Larry. Of course, in time Little Larry really grew to six foot something while his father stayed about five foot ten or maybe if he stood up straight, five eleven.

Some of my children who can remember some of these events tend to tell me that I have this or that detail wrong. And so I tell them what I now tell you, my readers, whoever you may be, that these memories are MINE, all mine.

My husband and I have seven children (really eight, but in those days we didn't count late term miscarriages). We have five boys and two girls. I have tried to restrict my writing to the early years since I think these wonderful kids deserve some privacy about their grownup lives. They will have to write the next chapters, perhaps each one to do their own.

FIRST COMMUNION

God, the Accountant

THERE ARE THOSE TODAY WHO MOCK AND MALIGN THE "GOOD NUNS" WHO TAUGHT US IN ELEMENTARY SCHOOL. They characterize them as mean and assaultive. My experience, all twelve years, was not that way at all. They were not soft and cuddly. They couldn't afford to be with 60 kids in a class. But they knew how to teach and teach us they did.

Our classes, while very large, were well behaved beyond today's belief. Why? Well, the nuns were not mean or violent but they did have God on their side.

God was not only part of religion class, God was everywhere, knew our most secret thoughts and desires and while I never trusted the priest's oath of secrecy in the confessional, I never doubted that God knew my every thought. For this I thank those nuns, for the sense of God has stayed with me and while it has grown and expanded and changed through prayer and study, God is as close as the next thought.

But in elementary school, God was *the accountant*, counting our good and bad deeds, entering them in some kind of huge book. Not that we were actually taught that, but that was my under-standing.

When occasions such as Mother's Day or Father's Day or Christmas or Easter would be coming we always would make a "Spiritual Bouquet" for mom or dad or both as the occasion dictated. What was a "Spiritual Bouquet"? Well, it first was a beautiful handmade card and inside was a personal message of love, but more impor-tant there was a list of good things we promised to do for the recipient - not like sweeping the floor or dusting the furniture. No. It listed the number of spiritual activities: Masses which we would offer for them, the number of rosaries we would say, the number of communions, the number of ejaculations.

Now, of course, that last word today is a little shocking, certainly in this context, but, of course, it didn't mean then what it means today. (Although, that's not a bad gift idea.) I am convinced that the nuns had no idea of the, should I say, "medical", no "sensual" meaning of the word and if enough of them lived long enough I am quite sure that they have had a few wonderful chuckles over that word and the "Bouquets".

To us, ejaculations were short prayers. There was a special one for Advent I still remember. "Oh Divine Babe of Bethlehem, whom the angels love and adore, come and take birth in our hearts".

Now each ejaculation was said quietly to one-self, while we were on line for the bathroom or whenever we had some free time while we waited for the class to finish and they were counted on our fingers. Each "Bouquet" would contain several thousand, especially since we had all four weeks of Advent to prepare for Christmas or seven weeks to get ready for Easter.

Now *the accountant* part involves yet another very important element that is no longer in vogue - that is indulgences. Each small prayer had a certain number of days or years attached and that meant that some soul's stay in Purgatory (we didn't deal with people who might be in hell) would be shortened by that many days.

It truly gave one a sense of great power and it focused our minds on God in all spare moments.

Part of being smart, and I was smart, was reading the small print in the back of the catechism. I found out early that a short ejaculation such as "Jesus, Mary and Joseph" had the same indulgence attached as the big one so I could really rack up the numbers. I was one of the best pray-ers going, if not the fastest.

But the real winner was a Plenary Indulgence which was granted very infrequently and let someone completely, instantly out of Purgatory and into Heaven.

Every Holy Thursday there was a Plenary Indulgence given every time you visited seven different churches and said three "Hail Mary's," three "Our Fathers" and three "Glory Be's". Since my father was a city cop and a terrible worrier, we weren't allowed outside our own neighborhood and could only go to our own church.

I can remember going one Holy Thursday to our church and going in and out after saying the mandatory prayers each time and figuring God didn't mind that I was sticking to one church. I will never forget a little old man stopping me in the vestibule (in those days we talked to little old men in the church vestibule). He said to me, "Little Girl, what are you doing?" He was smiling. I think I was angry at his smile and so I told him emphatically that I was freeing souls from Purgatory and sending them to Heaven.

With regard to regular indulgences I used to decide before I started whether I would send the soul closest to heaven out or work on the poor soul farthest away.

Of course, on Holy Thursday, when the indulgence was plenary it was always for the soul farthest and the one who had no one to pray for him. It was always a "him". We lived in a "him" world. God was a "him", the Spirit was a "him" and we girls were only created to keep Adam company and to have babies. (How, of course, I still didn't know.) But, by fifth grade I knew that the story of creation, while nice, was written by a man, so of course evil was brought into Paradise by a woman. If a woman had written it, the man would have said yes to the snake.

It was many years before I was courageous enough to speak these thoughts, but I am still a believer. God is very much present, no longer an *accountant*, but a loving "She" God and ejaculations have changed too. Wasn't God a clever one?

A Special Message

A
UNT ALICE WAS MY MOTHER'S PATERNAL AUNT.
She was John Powers', my grandfather's sister. An immigrant from Ireland, she worked as a serving girl for the Astors and there learned the "nice" things that she grew to want and indeed got when she could. Her husband, Jack, was a plain man, a taxi driver in New York City. I don't know whether or not he actually owned the medallion but I suspect that eventually he did. She was the only person who I knew as a child, who had a silver tea service, something I only knew from the movies. They lived on the West Side of Manhattan in an apartment that was always very fashionable by our standards or at least as fashionable as their income could afford. When we went there, there was always shrimp salad, an unheard of luxury. Over the years, the apartment stayed quite lovely as the neighborhood sagged and finally became a very dangerous place.

When they would come to visit, Aunt Alice would kind of swoop into my grandmother's house, dressed always to the nines, hat and white gloves, with their little yappy pooch under her arm. She would insist that she was exhausted from the trip, (they came by car from the West Side of Manhattan to Bay Ridge in Brooklyn) and needed a little something to relax her nerves. As soon as she had a shot of whiskey, neat, she would take her coat and gloves and hat off and would be ready to visit and have a high ball.

Aunt Alice had a history of "nerves". She had had a "nervous" breakdown after her first child, Jackie, was born, so severe that the doctors wanted to put her in a mental hospital. Her husband refused in spite of the fact that she was seeing little men crawling over the blankets at the foot of her bed. He insisted that he would take care of her at home and he did. It seems as though the second pregnancy cured her. And while she was always a little odd, she was really fine for as long as we knew her except for her exotic history.

They had two children, boys eighteen months a part, Jackie and Walter. The Second World War started the year that Jackie turned eighteen and he immediately enlisted. He was shipped to North Africa after a brief period of training and quickly was reported taken prisoner of war. Walter, by this time was old enough to enlist and did and shortly after, Jackie was reported killed in action. It was terrible.

While there was no body, there was a full blown wake and funeral. The family, recognizing the horror of losing a son and then having a second son going to war so soon and knowing Aunt Alice's history, was worried about her stability, but she was surprisingly steady in spite of Walter slogging through Europe with Patton's Tank Corps. Until that is about 1943, when she started to report dreams, dreams in which the Sacred Heart of Jesus would appear to her and tell her that He had a special message for her. These dreams were recurrent and became more and more frequent. As a child these reports frightened me. Was she crazy? Was she a saint like those in the religion books? Was Jesus really appearing to her? What was the message?

And then it happened. One night in 1944, Aunt Alice was awakened by a phone call from a man in Texas. He told her that he had just heard her son Jackie broadcasting shortwave from Germany and asking if anyone, anywhere could hear his voice to please call his mother in New York City. He gave the telephone number and said to tell her that he was alive and okay. And so this stranger called Aunt Alice. I don't think she even thought to ask his name, she was so excited. This was the message that Jesus had promised. She didn't need confirmation. She never doubted that it actually was her Jackie speaking to that stranger from Germany after four long years of being "dead".Shortly thereafter the War Department wrote to her and confirmed that her son, Jackie, was alive and a prisoner of war. The war ended and Jackie came home jaundiced for months from all the raw potatoes that he had survived on for the last four years. When he was captured, he was a strong, strapping, young man and instead of being sent to a camp, he was transported to a farm in Germany to work. It saved his life and we never again made fun of Aunt Alice or her strange and eccentric ways or her devotion to the Sacred Heart of Jesus.

The Highlands

EVERY YEAR MY SISTER, JOAN, AND I WOULD GO OFF TO THE COUNTRY, HIGHLANDS, N.J., to spend the summer "taking care of" or really "keeping my Grandmother company". She was barely five foot and maybe 95 pounds. She suffered from pleurisy. The country was supposed to be good for her, but my mom's sister and brother who lived with her, Aunt Kay and Uncle Bill, both worked and my father worked around the clock as a New York City Police Officer, so the perfectly wonderful job of taking care of Nana fell to my sister and me. The country was supposed to be good for us too in those days of polio and other diseases.

We generally did keep her company, but in truth my memories of those summers, and they went on for the next fifteen years, were of glorious freedom to come and to go, to offer to go downtown (the town was really a rundown little single street next to the Shrewsbury River), to play in the nearby woods and generally to have a wonderful time. In Brooklyn, you see, my father worried about us and so we could play in the yard or driveway, but never in the street. I often think my dental difficulties are from roller skating on the sidewalk in Brooklyn. Highlands was heaven to us.

The Highlands house was a real house, not a bungalow. It had a front porch and rocking chairs and a back porch too. On the back porch was the ice box, the closest thing to a coffin for a giant, probably four feet high and six feet long. It was painted grey and every other day the ice man, a foreign little man, who was incredibly strong, would deliver either fifty or a hundred pound piece of ice, slung over his shoulder on a piece of burlap. And every day my sister or I would empty the pan that sat under it to catch the melting water.

The front of the ground floor was the living room and the back was divided into the kitchen and dining room. It even had an upstairs with three bedrooms and a large bathroom. Did I say we loved it? It was heaven to us Brooklyn kids. There were no locks on the doors. That part was a little scary.

The kitchen had a big, black, kerosene stove. Small though my grandmother was in stature, she was a hero. In our minds she was really courageous. Every morning she would light that monster. Somehow she would shake the upside-down kerosene bottle until it bubbled and then with the black stove lid at the ready she would light the match and the flames would whoosh and she would somehow get the lid on the hole and turn buttons and gadgets and we would have our fire for the day. Of course there was no hot water but we didn't mind. It took about ten kettles to even start a bath, and we only had two kettles, so by the time the last kettle came up the stairs any hope of a warm bath was gone. We did not mind the lack of regular baths.

We were close to the ocean but were never allowed to go there without an adult, so every weekend we went. The sand that has built up on Breezy Point is the sand that each year was eroding from the beach in Highlands, New Jersey, but for most of our years there was enough beach to enjoy the wonderful and frightening surf. Because the beach dropped off so sharply the waves were ferocious.

One day, when a cousin of my Nana's, Brother Croke, was visiting, we went with him and Kay and Bill to the ocean. He went out beyond the waves and then he took me out with him. He thought he was giving me a treat and I was too shy to admit my terror since I couldn't swim. When he was ready to have a swim he asked me if I could swim into the shore. Of course I lied and said yes and came as close to drowning as I ever hope to. Aunt Kay and Uncle Bill suddenly realized what was happening and rushed in to rescue me. I cannot think of another time when I ventured out beyond those waves.

My sister, Joan, went to work in Oppenheim Collins for the summer when she turned 16. I missed her terribly, but I made friends with a girl down the road, Adelaide Concannon. Adelaide's mother made the most heavenly blueberry dumplings which of course required that Adelaide and I go berry picking and it was in one of those briars that I met the one and only snake face to face. I seem to remember that was the end of berry picking for me. Adelaide always taunted me as a city slicker but I remained on the road rather than in the thicket where the best berries grew.

I remember the first time I saw the Highlands house. We went with Aunt Kay and Uncle Bill to see it. It was early spring and quite cold, and a long ride from Brooklyn, across the Sixty Ninth Street Ferry, through Staten Island and down to Highlands, New Jersey. There was no Jersey Turnpike, no big road through Staten Island. I think they rented the house that same day from Mrs. White, the owner, and rented it every year for many years thereafter and Mrs. White became a good friend as well as the landlord

I can still see the horse shoes that Bill and my father loved and the big old apple tree on the side of the house that Joan and I hated since we had to rake the rotten apples. What yellow jackets and bees they attracted!

While we had a lot of freedom there, there were of course, certain understood boundaries. During the week we would always ask permission from Nana to go downtown and she would always say yes and on weekends we'd ask Aunt Kay. But there was that one Sunday while Katie and Nana were cooking dinner that Joan decided on an adventure. We would go to the Twin Lights without asking. The Twin Lights were a double lighthouse located on top of the hill opposite the house where its beacon had lit the entrance to New York Harbor for many years. This was quite an escapade. We were sure that if we asked the answer would be no or that they would take us up there by car and that would be no fun. We had to go all the way down Peak Street hill and through an overgrown dirt path up the opposite hill to the Lights and suddenly as we thrilled to our accomplishment at the top, that voice from the distance was shrieking, "Joan! Mary!" We knew then what we had done.

We could see Aunt Kay and Uncle Bill on the porch of the house in the distance and we could hear the frantic fear in her screams, "Joan", "Mary" and we waved and waved and yelled and finally got their attention. She and Bill drove up to get us. She was not angry, just so relieved and I don't think I have ever been so sorry. I fell on the way down to meet them and Joan insisted that I

not cry and not tell. It was as though she too realized the enormity of what we had done and didn't
want to add to Katie's pain. Of course, at dinner,
as the blood continued to run down my leg, it was
discovered and she carefully and kindly bandaged
me up.

And then there were the parties at Galligan's.
Alice Galligan was a good friend of Katie's. She had
an interesting history: one of twenty one children
by one father and three mothers. Her half-sister,
Rose, ran the family sugar refining business which
prospered until the border with Cuba closed and
she was the one who owned the house down the
hill. Alice was disabled by childhood polio. She
had a severe limp and one arm couldn't extend
but Rose kept her employed in the family business. I feel myself digressing. So many stories!

Oh but what parties at the Galligans! And
Katie took us along! Rose was a big "priest" lady
and she used to serve Tom Collins in those tall
weekly votive candle glasses from church. Joan
and I thought this was scandalous!

It was the only time I ever heard Uncle Bill tell
stories of Ireland. I can remember the night he
told of going home after dark through the field
and finding a comb and hearing the cry of the
banshee. She was somewhere there combing her
long hair and wailing. It was not a good spirit, and
not really a bad one, but most assuredly a scary

one. I think it portended death. I can still feel the fright.

The morning after the parties, if there was a priest in attendance and there usually was, there would be a Mass in the Galligan's living room with big Uncle Bill, the altar 'boy'. It was some squeeze for him getting up and down from his knees in that tiny room. She even had a set of altar bells which he dutifully rang at the appropriate moments. I guess those were my first 'home Masses'.

Joan and I would be there all week with Nana and on Friday night Aunt Kay would come down on the train if Uncle Bill were working. We would trot down to the station, sometimes twice if she missed the early train. It was quite a walk, but there she'd be loaded with Horn & Hardart boxes, goodies for the weekend.

The Peach Taffeta Dresses

Each Easter, Aunt Kay would buy Joan and me new dresses. These were very special since new party-like dresses were not part of our usual wardrobe which consisted of uniforms for school, one outfit for Sunday Mass and then just plain play clothes. But Katie would engage in a "Tooth Fairy" like endeavor so that the dresses would be a surprise gift and still fit perfectly. She would tell us a few weeks before Easter that her friend Ann who had two nieces just about our ages wanted to buy them new dresses and could we possibly try them on for her to see if they would fit. Of course, knowing that the dresses were really for us, we gladly obliged.

The usual color scheme was pink or red for Joan, the brunette, and blue or green for me, the redhead. But that year the dresses were both peach. They were beautiful. They were taffeta. The feel of taffeta, the rustle, the sheen, I remember it as though it were today. They were different styles. Katie knew how I felt about wearing the same outfit as Joan and so while they were both peach they were different. I remember feeling like a princess and hoping that that year would be like the last time and that the dresses were really for us. And while there were many dresses over the years, that year about which I speak is imprinted in my memory as though it were yesterday. I think I was not yet in school. It was a very long time ago.

We were at our grandmother's, in the dining room. It was a big room. The sun was streaming in. She lived on the second floor. Her dining room table was quite large in the fashion of the times. We had put the dresses on and were there modeling them so that Aunt Kay could see whether or not they fit, Oh how I loved that dress! My mom and Katie both were commenting on how wonderful the peach looked on both of us.

And then something happened. I don't know what started it but my mother got very angry at Joan. So angry that she reached out for her and Joan started to run away, around the dining room table she went with my mom in pursuit. And then Mom grabbed her and the dress ripped right down the back. It was a most horrible, frightening thing. How could she ruin that dress? Why did Joan provoke her? I knew it was the end of the peach taffeta dresses, mine too and the saddest moment of my young life. It was sad, but it was also really frightening, the sight of rage up close and very personal. My mom was out of control, over what? I don't remember. What I do remember is that gorgeous peach taffeta dress that I never saw again.

Secrets

O N AUGUST 26TH, 1940, I WAS SEVEN YEARS OLD. Joan and I had spent the summer in Highlands, New Jersey, with Kay and Bill and Nana. Uncle Bill was driving us home to our house in Bay Ridge, Brooklyn, 672 71st Street. It was a beastly hot day and so the family and neighbors were all out sitting on the front stoop. As we drove up I suddenly noticed my mother. Oh my God! She was huge, like something from a monster fairytale. She was almost unrecognizable. What was wrong with her? I remember being terribly frightened. What had happened to her over the summer? She hadn't come up to the country that year but there were always excuses that sounded credible. But here she was almost unable to stand.

The next day my mom said she was going to lay down since she didn't feel well; a very rare, actually a never before kind of thing. She told us we could wash our dollies' clothes in the kitchen sink, another never before kind of thing. And then suddenly she called out to us from the bedroom that we were to call Mrs. Hellings, our upstairs neighbor. Something was terribly wrong. In a short time a police car brought my father home, another never before kind of thing and we were whisked off to our grandmother's house. That night we slept in Aunt Kay's bed. It was a little scary because at the foot of her bed was a picture of Our Lady of Perpetual Help that had eyes that followed you wherever you went. Joan and I used to test it. She would go to the window and I to the door but those eyes would be following both of us. But there was nary a word about our mother or what had happened.

The next morning Aunt Kay greeted us with the news, "You have a new baby brother!" BIG, BIG SECRET! Where did he come from? How did he get here? What was going on? She told us that we would return to the country for the last two weeks of summer. Secrets! Secrets! Why deny two little girls the pleasure, the delight, the anticipation of a new baby? I don't know and I never asked. What is even stranger is the fact that I never asked my sister, Joan, these questions. Did she know? I don't know. I think that we were trained to not ask. Not actually told just somehow given the message.

A few months later a girl, Joan Anderson, who frequently visited across the street and played with me when she came, told me that her mom had just told her that babies came out of a hole between the mom's legs. I was appalled at her stupidity and of course did not believe her.

And when our beautiful baby brother, Edward, named after my father, was changed it was always in private, we never saw those male parts. Although we knew there was something hidden there, some reason to hide something we didn't know what and we didn't dare ask. And so when I write about secrets maybe I should title this memoir *Sick Secrets*. What in the name of all that's good and sensible were we being protected from?

Joan and I used to be allowed to take the baby, Edward, for short strolls. Of course we would fight over who was holding the handle and where we were going and then one day as we fussed with each other and pushed and pulled, the carriage tipped over and Edward bounced out backwards. I know that his head hit the sidewalk because I can still hear it. But the harness that attached him to the carriage must have saved him from a really hard hit. And of course, we never told. It was our secret. There was no blood and he quickly stopped crying and he seems to have turned out very well so I guess it wasn't as bad as we thought.

Recently as a result of a Jungian Retreat, Edward, now a De La Salle Christian Brother, Uncle Brother to the kids, asked me if Joan and I ever played with him when he was little since he has no recollection of that. Actually as I thought about it, I had no memory of playing with him either other than the carriage incident. When he was really little Joan and I would take him for rides in the infamous carriage and later in the stroller. I was seven years older, but nevertheless I should have had some memories of playing with him, reading stories, doing puzzles or something. But I don't. But as I thought about this I realized that as soon as he was big enough to really play, it was my father who played with him, boy games, catch and things like that. Dad would coach Little League Teams, taking the whole team down to Shore Road to the fields there in our old jalopy and then taking the whole bunch of kids to the candy store for a treat each.

I recently found a very old birthday card from my brother to "Daddy" signed "Your Buddy, Edward". I think they really were buddies and that my father provided a loving shield as best he could from the harshness of my mother's growing addiction. Did I say my mother was becoming an alcoholic? Another big secret!

Threads

IWAS SIXTEEN, TALL, AND THIN, WITH BRIGHT RED HAIR. I lived in Bay Ridge, Brooklyn and went to school in Park Slope and I had my first job. It was at JOHN WANAMAKER'S on Eighth Street in Manhattan. It was part time, Thursday nights and Saturdays from nine to five. The department stores were closed on Sundays then. As a part timer it was my job to fill in for all different departments wherever needed, sometimes working as the maître d' (what is the feminine of that word?), at the little café/coffee bar in the basement, and at other times in the stationery department, etc.

Then one fateful Saturday I was assigned to the bed linens department. I figured that I would spend my day refolding the merchandise and that it would be a really slow day. As a part timer I worked on salary. I can't really remember the amount but seem to think it was very small.

And then this elderly gentleman approached me and asked, "Can you help me, young lady?"

"Of course, yes sir, what can I do for you?"

"Well I need some help on these sheets. I want to buy some sheets and I have some questions."

"Well," I replied, "I am only part time and those ladies over there are the regular sales ladies and I am sure they can help you and answer all your questions." The regular sales people worked on commission and were already giving me that kind of penetrating stare that told me in no uncertain terms that I was not to take this sale, but to no avail.

He insisted. "I want you to help me."

"Well, Sir, how can I help then?"

"I want to know how many threads there are in these sheets." He held up a package. For a moment I was about to laugh. What a silly question! Was he teasing me, trying to make me feel foolish or what?

I think my shyness saved me from outright laughter as I said, "Well I really don't know how many threads there are in that sheet, but I will find out. Are you sure you don't want the regular salesgirl to help you?"

"No. I already told you I want you to help me."

"Okay, I will find out."

Then I had to face the regular saleswoman who by now was clearly furious and I had to ask this stupid question. But I did and she answered through clinched teeth that there were 350 threads and it was clearly marked on the side of the package. I returned to the gentleman and told him and he with my "help" picked out a pile of sheets, 350 threads each, whatever that meant. The total sale was about four hundred dollars, a staggering amount to me and I daresay to the regular saleswoman as well.

I never was assigned to the bed linens department again. And now when I lay on my 350 or 400 thread sheets, especially on Fridays when they are freshly ironed, I always remember my first job and how naïve I was and how far I have come, at least when it comes to bed sheets.

Bellyache

MY FATHER WAS A NEW YORK CITY COP FOR TWENTY SEVEN YEARS. In one way he hated the police having grown up as an orphan on the streets of New York, but in another way he loved it. He was instrumental in helping form the first Patrolmen's Benevolent Association (PBA) for city cops for which he was accused of being a Red, a Commie, a Union organizer, as well as other choice epithets when the police were supposed to be above all that.

But "bellyache" was a favorite expression of his to which my mom always objected claiming it was crude. "Don't bellyache," became a family mantra in the vein of stop complaining, no whining.

My second real job came in the summer between high school and college. I had spent that whole spring looking for something in order to save some much needed money, but was unsuccessful. Each time when the job recruiter would ask about college in the fall and I said that I would be going that would be the end of any offer, only filing jobs remained and they paid very little.

When I saw an ad from Sacony Vacuum Oil Company for a rather well paid filing job I applied, but only after deciding that truth was not the better part of valor. What harm would it be to hold back on the truth, after all, it was only a filing job, nothing serious, a kind of little white lie.

So I applied and when they asked about school, I said that I could not afford to go, which in a rather twisted way was actually true. I was on the job only a week when I realized the enormity of my transgression. This was not a filing job, but rather a kind of archival librarian job, a kind of old fashioned Google like job. The office was divided into sections of the world where Sacony Vacuum had business and we each had a desk for that geographical area. I was assigned to the Middle East. When an executive wrote a letter or memo regarding different subjects it was our job to index it first by main subject using a Dewey Decimal type system and then to cross reference it to any other subject that was mentioned.

It was fascinating to read the correspondence about the oil pipelines, the Sheiks, the financial implications and transactions with the various governments in an area of the world that was new and exotic to me, to learn from one of the very experienced ladies the numbering system and then to participate in the sometimes frantic search for the particular letter that some Vice President wanted in which he remembered mentioning something about this or that. It was a little like that movie with Katherine Hepburn and Spencer Tracy and the first "Big Blue" computer that was trying to replace a group of ladies very much like my colleagues.

It only took two weeks for the "bellyache" to get so bad that I ended up with my very first x-rays. With the wisdom of age I now know that what was wrong with my stomach was, of course, GUILT. But at that time I lacked courage and needed the money and it was such a wonderful job. At lunch we would go outside to listen to the big bands that played at the Battery Park. The music would reverberate up Broadway echoing off the skyscrapers.

As the summer was coming to an end I had to tell them that I was leaving to go to college and so I told them another lie, really a big half-truth. I had won a scholarship to St. John's Teachers' College and so could afford to go. This was true but only half since I had won the scholarship early in April.

I think the worst part was that they were so nice to me, congratulating me and wishing me well and then to top it all off, they gave me a going away party.

That bellyache lasted a long time.

WEDDING PICTURE, MARCH 5, 1955– FROM L. TO R. ED
MCCORMACK, RUTH DOLAN, LARRY AND MARY, JOAN,
GEORGE WERNER, BESSIE WERNER, AND DONALD WERNER

The First Wife

MY HUSBAND HAS ALWAYS INTRODUCED ME AS HIS SIXTH WIFE. So I guess in writing my memoirs I best start with wife number one.

The Saint John's College/Teachers' College building was very old and the stairs were white marble, the kind that has wavy indentations in the middle from the thousands of feet that have trod them. My hands were full of books and, as I started down, there he was, thin, no – really skinny; horn rimmed glasses. I had my eye on him for a while but no conversation. He was very quiet. As I looked at him I slipped and fell down the stairs and he caught me. And, of course, ever since, he has said "What a good catch."

We talk about love at first sight but I am convinced there is something between two people that draws them inexorably together. Suddenly school was not so important and he was on his way to medical school and we were both really Catholic (translation: no sex before marriage) and so, in short order we decided to get married. The wedding was held at St. Ephraim's Church on March 5th, 1955, the reception at Michel's in Park Slope.

I quit school. I didn't really know what I wanted to be anyway. We were all headed to becoming teachers; not for any reason of thought out desire but it was what the girls did; safe, secure, a job you could always go back to and a pension at the end.

So I quit college to work so he could go to med school. I didn't see it as a sacrifice; it was just the way it was going to be. And when we moved into a tiny furnished tenement in the city I think I felt heroic or something, at least until I found the cockroaches in my lingerie drawer and my mother-in-law suggesting I inspect the mattress for bed bugs. I can remember my horror. "What are they? What do they look like, these bedbugs?"

She explained how I should inspect the edge of the mattress by the ticking and that they were very small and black and hard to see.

Funny story: I had a small female thing that required a visit to the doctor and there was this very young, very handsome OB/GYN Doctor whose name was William J. Sweeney III and he didn't charge medical school wives. So after he examined me he directed me into his office and the conversation went something like this. A prescription for my little problem and, "Oh, is there anything else?"

I had never met someone who was a third anything, so I was a little intimidated but I soldiered on and told him that actually I was a little worried that I was not yet pregnant. His face was - how can I say it? Surprised, amused.

"How long have you been married? he said with a little smirk.

"Oh" I said, "five months and I was worried something was wrong."

At that point he could no longer resist, he just laughed outright and said, "You might be... just." and so I went home happy as a clam.

Then came my battle with the roaches. I was determined. I went to the drugstore and asked the pharmacist for something to kill the critters. In hindsight it seems very strange that I did not go to a hardware store, but a pharmacy. We were living on East 82nd Street in Manhattan in a six story walk-up and I don't remember any hardware stores in that neighborhood. He gave me something and advised me to use it undiluted on the baseboards and on the dish closet shelves and to put it in the wash water for the linoleum floors. It was Chlordane, something I now know to be a highly toxic poison, but I was thrilled because it worked. How stupid we were. I was pregnant and stroked that stuff on big time.

The baby arrived, Little Larry, a month early. He was not a sleeper at least not ever at night (maybe it was the Chlordane) and my husband had to study and so my nights were spent with rocking and trying to lower the baby into the crib. I think he had some kind of weird radar that woke him as soon as he was in the vicinity of the crib mattress. By day we did the battle of the carriage. The neighborhood was not the kind of place you could leave the carriage down stairs and so I would race the baby and the groceries up to the apartment and then leave the baby screaming in the crib to race down and bounce the carriage up the four flights. We had the inside apartment. It had windows but you couldn't see anything because it was on an areaway, about ten feet wide so neither rain nor sun nor snow penetrated down far enough for us to see.

Thirteen months later the second baby, Kevin, arrived. By then we had moved to Flatbush since my husband was going to do his internship at King's County Hospital. This one was also not a sleeper; actually I would put him in the screamer category. But he had cause: he came home from New York Hospital with a staph infection and needed several weeks of antibiotics, and then he broke out in a rash, that was totally resistant to all the usual treatments. He was about nine months when on a regular checkup visit, the doctor offered me a tube with many dire warnings: it was new, be very careful, don't use too much, etc. Two days later the rash was gone. The tube was cortisone cream. The year was 1957-58. It was a miracle! While the cream cured his rash, however, I think he had gotten used to not sleeping. But the apartment in Flatbush, while in a basement had windows in the back that allowed the sun in and a fenced-in backyard with grass. Life was getting better.

During third year medical school my husband got involved (I think you might call it enlisted, but it was not a usual enlistment process) with the Air Force. They paid him as a Second Lieutenant, the next year as a First Lieutenant and finally as a Captain and all he had to do was to put on a uniform once a year, go out to Mitchell Air Force Base and get sworn in. He then was obligated, of course, to give them back year for year after he finished his medical training.

He was doing his internship at King's County and I had just had my third baby, Steven, who was an angel child. He slept in the bassinet beside the washing machine in the kitchen which was going nonstop with three babies in diapers. Maybe that was why he was such a good sleeper.

My mom was with me helping out. We were anxiously awaiting our orders to find out where we would spend the next six years. The bell rang. The postman used to do that, ring the bell. But that day he had a big package and it was from the Air Force. Oh what excitement! I opened the envelope. There were one hundred copies of

Larry's orders which was standard operating procedure with the Air Force. But I couldn't understand them, all of those numbers and letters.

My mom said, "Mary, just sit down and read them out loud slowly. We can figure them out."

So I started and in the middle of the first paragraph there it was: "APO San Francisco, California." Oh I was elated. I had never been west of New Jersey. California! Fantastic! But for some reason my mother had started to cry.

"What's wrong? California is not so far."

She blubbered through her sobs, "No Mary you are going further than California"

"How do you know that?"

"I remember from the War writing to the boys. That's what APO means, Air Post Office." She urged me to look further in the envelope. And there it was. No more than a 5x7 inch booklet. It had a picture of a water buffalo on the cover and said "Welcome to the Philippine Islands" and then I started to cry.

"Where are they?" she said, "the Philippine Islands? Look in the dictionary."

In that little furnished apartment strangely enough there was a dictionary. "A cluster of islands off the coast of China", it said. I think I cried for a week.

It is a very little known fact that the Philippine Islands are as far from Brooklyn as you can go without coming back. But worse yet, in the packet was a letter saying I couldn't go with him, something about housing. Bad as the thought of the Philippine Islands was, I knew that him going and me staying in Flatbush with the three babies was unacceptable.

A second letter arrived shortly advising that housing had been arranged for us there and that we should go to the Surgeon General with that letter and get new orders. Who knew the Surgeon General? Go to Washington? Impossible!

Well, we did. Mom watched the two older ones and we took the baby to Washington in one of those cardboard boxes the hospital used to give new moms and we saw Washington for the first time - from the car that is. We drove around and around. Washington is that kind of a city. There was no parking anywhere, there was no intelligible street grid, round and round we went. We finally found the Surgeon General's Office and a Corporal Radar O'Reilly kind of guy told Larry, Captain Werner, to come back after lunch and he would cut him new orders so we could go together.

And he did and so that summer I spent taking the three babies into Fort Hamilton in Brooklyn for shots that made us all awfully sick and my husband went to Georgia and learned to salute and actually fired a gun twice, I think. Labor Day weekend we all went out to Idlewild Airport (now known as Kennedy International Airport) and got on a plane for California and then on to the Philippine Islands and so ends Wife Number 1.

The Me

IN WRITING MY MEMORIES I AM SUDDENLY STRUCK BY THE FACT THAT I STARTED WITH MY FALLING DOWN THE STAIRS INTO THE ARMS OF MY HUSBAND TO BE, AT NINETEEN. But there was a "me" before there was an "us" and the "me" is who I am while the "us" is who I have become. So....

I was born on June 1, 1933, at Victory Memorial Hospital in Brooklyn, N.Y. the second child of Alice Powers and Edward L. Phelan. I had an older sister, Joan, and seven years later I had a brother, Brother Edward. All four of my grandparents were born in Ireland, but my mom's parents, while working immigrants were alive and well and she graduated from Bay Ridge High School and got a job as a secretary and worked for the next ten years.

My father never went further than eighth grade. He was an orphan whose mom died when he was four and his father when he was ten, leaving a family of six children. He was brought up by two older sisters and always remembered the way the kids were instructed never to open the door especially to the aunts since they only wanted to put all of them in an orphanage. He never knew whether or not this was true but he often told of the many apartments in lower Manhattan where they lived for a few months, the first free and then only until the landlord could throw them out for non-payment which was a whole lot easier then than it is today.

My sister was three years older than I, with dark curly hair, very smart. She had the kind of hair that when you put those big taffeta bows in they stayed. I, on the other hand, was red haired and freckled. My hair was so thin it refused to hold even bobby pins let alone those magnificent bows.

It's funny how things affect you years after the fact. When my mom died and my sister and I were going through her few things we came across "Joan's Baby Book", replete with all those endearing pictures and memories of her first words, and her visits to her, "Joan's Beach" known to everyone else as Jones Beach. There wasn't a Mary's Baby Book nor was there a book for Edward. The feelings that engendered are still truly unscrambled especially since as the mother of seven I had no time to do even that first "Baby Book".

We went to Catholic School, Our Lady of Angels (OLA). Officially we were in St. Ephraim's Parish but my mom had visited their school and thought the first grades located in the basement were dangerously damp. Our grandmother lived on Senator Street and that was in the OLA parish and so for eight years, while going to Catholic School, we lied every time we were asked our address and dutifully said we lived at Senator Street. Actually it was a good thing because we had to go to confession at least every two weeks and the only sins I could think of were those times that I had to write my address. Interesting thought: even as children we were taught about the seal of confession which meant that nothing you told the priest there was ever to be divulged by him. As I look back now I realize that I didn't really believe that since I never told him just what the lie was that I was confessing for fear he would tell and we would be thrown out of our school.

I said that Joan was smart, the smartest in her class and, of course, I had to be likewise. One of the proudest moments in my young life was when I grew taller than she and she had to wear my hand me downs instead of me wearing hers. When it was time for high school all I knew was that I wanted to go to a different school than she attended so that there would be a stop to the comparisons that haunted me all through grammar school, so off to Saint Saviour's High School in Park Slope I went.

My mother was an alcoholic and that fact influenced my life probably more than any other. She was an Irish secret drinker. The liquor store delivered and when a drink was offered socially she frequently refused, but on any given day I knew as soon as I got home from school whether or not she had been drinking. She would just not be my mother, but someone else who I didn't like.

Was that a factor in my early marriage to a guy in second year medical school who had no money? Was that a factor in my young brother's joining the Brothers at fifteen and going away to Barrytown? Was that a factor in my father's coming home one day and announcing he would never have another drink? Of course it was, but what has subsequently become a more brilliant factor in my life is my admiration for my mother who stopped drinking at around age fifty nine, no AA, no group therapy, no nothing just pure determination. How hard it must have been. But as I said before we were Irish so we never talked about it, the drinking or the stopping. And so instead I am writing about it.

How Wrong Was Wrong

WE'RE AT THE AIRPORT, IDLEWILD; IT'S DARK PROBABLY NINE OR TEN O'CLOCK; THE WHOLE FAMILY IS THERE TO SEND US OFF; TEARS; OH GOD, HOW I WISHED THAT THIS PART WOULD JUST BE OVER, LET US JUST GET ON THAT PLANE AND THINGS WILL BE OK.

And so on we got. Relief! Well not really, but everyone strapped into their seats and the engines started. When you are really busy you don't have time or energy to think of what you are actually terrified of. Flying, that is or was. But I held on tight, said my Act of Contrition (I still do that) and kept telling myself that the bumps and noises were no more than the Fourteenth Street Subway. When I turned to my husband and said well that was not too bad he smiled and said we hadn't even taken off yet. We were just taxiing. Even then that airport was huge.

As soon as we took off the lights were turned off or turned down low, it was a night time flight and most of the passengers were prepared to sleep. And even I, in my naiveté, thought my little angels would sleep. I dressed them in their pajamas thinking that would fool them. But the two oldest, two and a half and one and a half, didn't sleep at home so I don't know what I was thinking when I prepared them to sleep on the plane. And as we ascended into the night sky to however many thousand feet, the plane got cold and I had the babies in their summer pj's because it was Labor Day weekend, hot in New York and we were going to the Philippines which was going to be hot and on the way we would fly into Hawaii which would be hot and then onto other tropical islands. You see the logic of summer pj's?

Of course the older two, Larry and Kevin, were prepared to frolic; they soon realized what fun it would be to try to untie the shoes of the sleeping passengers as they, the kids that is, crawled under the seats while my husband tried to coral them quietly and I held the baby, Steven, who up to that very day was a wonderful sleeper, but as it turned out he was suffering from an earache and the altitude was very painful and he was screaming. I thought that when we landed in San Francisco we would have to get him to a doctor. Funny, my husband, the doctor, was right there beside me but I didn't think of him as a real doctor, at least not yet.

As the night wore on and the stewardess kept telling us to keep the children in their seats and the baby cried, I called the stewardess over and asked could we order drinks.

"Of course", she said. "What can I get you?"

"Three Manhattans ", I said. "The boys will share one". And they did and eventually we all slept.

As daylight dawned, the pilot announced that we would be landing in San Francisco soon and that it was seven thirty in the morning and the temperature was fifty one degrees. At that moment I realized that something had gone awry with my planning. And so my husband and I decided that we would let all the passengers get off and then we would try to gather all our stuff and then take the next step, whatever that was. I had gotten each of the boys a little bag for them to put their favorite toys and crayons and stuff in to carry on which was another idea gone sour since in about two minutes they were thoroughly bored with their things and then the bags were just another thing for the two of us to carry with the baby and two toddlers.

I am a firm believer in God and just as the last passenger passed us by with that kind of a 'boy am I glad I wasn't sitting closer to you all look' an older gentleman (God sent) stopped and asked us if we were being met at the airport, which of course we weren't and then he offered to take us to a motel for us to rest up and figure out our next step. He was a professor at UCLA and took us out to Berkeley to a motel where we got our bearings and slept and found a "real" doctor to look at

Steven and rented a car and got Steven the medicine and then drove out to Travis Air Base thinking we would be on the afternoon flight.

How wrong is wrong!!

The Point of No Return

WE THOUGHT THAT ONCE WE GOT TO TRAVIS WE WOULD TAKE THE NEXT FLIGHT OUT TO HAWAII THAT AFTERNOON. I remember being in the office of someone in uniform who was obviously important since he told us that there was something wrong with my passport. I had had it taken care of months before but what I didn't realize was that the picture on the passport was only of me and the two older children since when we had the picture taken Steven was not yet born. So we had to go into San Francisco and have another picture taken of me and the three children and then go to the passport office and do all that paper work again.

The officer behind the desk was so sweet when he told me that that it would probably take a couple of days but not to worry we, that is me and the three babies, could stay in the dormitory for women and children and my husband could stay in the BOQ, the Bachelors Officers Quarters. A private room just for him!!!! If that had happened to me now they would have had to call the Military Police and the ambulance because I would have been screaming so loud that they would have put me in restraints. But in looking back I can begin to understand how people comply with the most ridiculous demands when tired and young and just plain stupid. And when those commands are given by someone in uniform compliance comes even easier.

We still have the passport picture that we took that day and in the background is the top of my husband's head. He was holding Kevin by the seat of his pants. And he, Kevin, that is, was wearing one of those harnesses that we would use. It kept him from killing himself or running off. Young moms today consider them abusive, almost as bad as playpens. They call them dog leashes but the kids were always at the other end and safe.

And so we spent the next couple of days back in the motel, driving back and forth to San Francisco and to the Base and finally when we were just about out of money (no credit cards then) we were told that we were on the next flight to Hawaii, Hickam Air Base. Now, no longer commercial, we were traveling Military Air Transport a/k/a MATS. There were advantages and disadvantages: the stewardess was a steward, a nice guy who didn't care if the kids romped up and down the aisle and the other passengers were mostly single guys who thought the kids were cute and if not cute at least tolerable.

I didn't mention that if you know about the alignment of the stars and the moon and the sun and if you are traveling by propeller aircraft going at a certain speed then if you start in the dark you can fly forever in the dark. And we did. And the disadvantage of MATS travel was the plane had no insulation and was very loud and I don't remember any food or drink. I seem to think there were box lunches.

The flight took about twelve hours and halfway through the pilot, in his most serious, I would say sonorous, voice, announced "WE HAVE NOW PASSED THE POINT OF NO RETURN" Boy was he right!

We landed in Hickam and were told that we should go to the cafeteria and eat and there was a nice nursery for the babies. There are moments in life that we remember and regret, and my leaving my three babies in that nursery is one of them, but I was saved because before we could even start eating our food they announced that our flight was departing. Suddenly things seemed to be in a hurry. So off to the flight line and into the darkness and again the NO RETURN message. God, how I hated that!

The next stop, Kwaljulaine, was a beautiful atoll in the middle of the Pacific Ocean. It was actually daylight when we landed. We were what must have been about a week and a half sleep deprived, exhausted, dirty and only half way there, but my husband called me over to a doorway in the lounge where we were waiting for our flight and he showed me a beautiful scene, a small mound with three crosses and some palm trees a short distance off shore. It was a memorial to three army nurses who gave their lives during the War. It could only be described as a picture postcard.

Knowing I was close to the breaking point he tried to assure me that we were ok and we would make it. I had one change of clothing for the babies and me left. My poor husband was still in the same uniform he was in when we left Brooklyn. So I changed the babies and then went into a small bathroom to shower and change and try to put on a fresh, optimistic attitude. It had started to rain and in the tropics when it rains it really rains. A strange thing happened when I turned the shower off the water kept coming and in short order I realized that in the Orient windows can't be closed because of the intense, all powerful heat and so the rain was coming through the open slats of the window. I quickly dressed and returned to the lounge where the boys were happily sloshing through the water which by then was about two inches on the floor.

And so for the first, the only time in my life, before or since, I fainted. I had the sense to fall on a couch. I remember voices, excited, "She's fainted! Get a doctor!" and my husband calmly saying "She's fine, leave her alone" and then as the frenzy picked up he said, "I am a doctor, let her rest." And then the announcement came, to report to the flight line. Time to go. And he was right. I was fine.

The Typhoon

A S WE RUSHED TO THE FLIGHT LINE THE RAIN WAS COMING VERY HEAVY AND THE WIND WAS FERO-CIOUS. We were on our way and into the darkness again. But this time the flight was very rough. We bounced and rocked in the air. Turbulence doesn't really describe the fury of the storm. We were like an empty box being tossed on a turbulent sea.

The three babies all went to sleep (it was the first time since we left NY, first time at least all together) and most of the sailors and airmen on board used the "barf bags". The smell was horrendous, but not important. We were going to die so what did that matter. It was terrifying! To think that this huge plane could stay up in the air and not literally blow apart was beyond belief. Just when we thought the worst was over, you sensed that the engines had suddenly stopped and the plane would drop, not nose down but flat out like a belly flop down, down, down, like a speeding elevator out of control. What is it that I feared so much? Dying?

We were all together and if we went I didn't have to worry who would take care of the children. But all the belief in God, all the rationalizations

didn't seem to work. Just terror! When I figured
we were about to crash, the plane's engines would
sound like they had started up again and the
plane would take off, up this time like the same
furious elevator coming to its senses. This went
on for the whole trip to Guam which was our next
stop. I think it was about ten hours.

In Guam the place was a frenzy of planes landing, everyone trying to get out of the storm and
onto the ground. It was a typhoon. No one had
mentioned that word up to that point. We were
herded into a huge hanger, given instructions
that no one could hear because of the rain on the
metal roof and then into buses and out to a Quonset hut where someone magically produced milk
for the babies and diapers. I am not sure which was
more important at that moment. We were given a
room with five beds and they all slept while I lay
there watching the rain come in through the slats
in the windows on one side of the room and blow
across us and out the other side. What kept that
Quonset hut on the ground that night I will never
know.

Morning finally came. The sun shone. The
palm trees glistened. We had breakfast and then
back on board, this time to the Philippines, our
final destination and again into the darkness.
Eight hours later we landed and were met by
friendly faces. Doctors assigned to the hospital

were there to greet us and told us that the Colonel wanted us to come to his house. We were in the Air Force and he was the Commanding Officer so, of course, we went to the Colonel's house.

In the service, people travel every couple of years to new assignments and when they are in exotic places they collect all sorts of beautiful and some not so beautiful tchatchkes and that Colonel's house was full of them and my two toddlers were like caged animals let loose after a long imprisonment. They must have touched every single thing on every single table. Quickly, the Colonel suggested that we might want to go to our off base quarters and rest.

Service people are really very nice. They try to take care of newcomers as best they can especially until the arrival of one's things which took six weeks. They had rented a house in Balibago for us that was quite nice. There were mattresses for each of us in the bedroom on the floor since they assumed that our furniture would be arriving soon. We quickly lay our weary heads down and slept. That is they slept while I watched this lizard like creature crawl across the ceiling right over our heads. As a Brooklyn girl who had lived with cockroaches in East Eighty Second Street I should have known that whatever creatures New York City produced the tropics produce bigger and better. Now thanks to an ad campaign, we know this little bugger as a friendly gecko. It didn't look so friendly to me that night.

Kevin, our second, who was not a real good sleeper, woke us as dawn came. Larry and I decided we would get up and try to let the other two sleep as long as possible. We went out into the living room with him and tried to pretend that normal life was about to begin. The living room had two straight back chairs and all the remains of the bags of toys. So as we sat there and Kevin played and we tried to take in our new surroundings, we suddenly realized that the large picture window that looked out on a small front yard was filled with a huge creature that was disturbingly familiar, a water buffalo. I recognized him from that leaflet that came with our orders those many months and thousands of miles ago. It was munching on the morning glories that were growing on the fence. It was on our side of the fence.

Welcome to the Philippine Islands.

Death Be Not Proud

"HOW DID YOU LIKE THE PHILIPPINE ISLANDS", SO MANY PEOPLE HAVE ASKED OVER THE YEARS. "What was it like?"

It was like being in a rather well run federal prison, the kind where the really well connected mobsters get to go.

It was hot, very hot and wet - green fuzzy mold would grow on shoes, books and luggage over-night. There were bugs, big humongous bugs and poisonous snakes, cobras lived in our backyard where I used to put the baby out in his playpen at least until we saw the cobra.

We discovered the cobra when my husband, Larry, was watering the patch of dry frazzled grass that was our backyard and when he absentmind-edly aimed the hose into what he thought was an ant hole, up popped a rather large hooded cobra which he instinctively shot with the hose and which then popped up from another hole and thus ended the backyard as a playground for the boys and soon after that we were moved to "on Base" housing which was a vast improvement. On Base they sprayed so much insecticide that cobras and even a lot of cockroaches didn't survive.

Until that moment the memos that we had received about how long one had from snake bite to anti-venom and how the location on the body of the bite and the speed with which one got oneself to the hospital for the venom was so important to one's survival, were just more Air Force formalities. Not after that.

Our first house was "off base". We got our stuff (cribs, strollers, high chair, clothes, toys, dishes, bikes) after about six weeks. It was shipped in containers by sea. But then my husband's next orders also arrived: four weeks temporary duty, TDY, to Taipei, some small missile base in the isolated north which obviously needed to have a doctor. It should be noted that the primary illness there in the P.I. as well as in Taipei, was venereal disease such that my husband never even mentioned that he had seen someone we knew at the clinic. He maintained that rule all his professional life, but would relent if someone we both knew died. How many times did I feel foolish when someone I knew well would ask hadn't Larry told me of their latest health problem or hospitalization.

We'd arrived mid-September and his orders took him to Taipei until mid-December. The Christmas trees arrived while he was gone. I had always said that our first Christmas tree was the saddest, a real "Charlie Brown" affair, but that was before we arrived in the P.I. and I had to stand on line in the simmering heat for an hour to take home a branch that they had the nerve to call a Christmas tree that had been flown in from California.

But all this is on the negative side of the register. On the positive side we were living in a real house for the first time. We bought our own furniture for the first time, rattan, cheap but very nice. I designed Philippine mahogany chests and tables which still sit in our "playroom" in Smithtown. They are still there partly because Philippine mahogany is among the densest wood, i.e. the heaviest, so once placed, there is a very strong tendency to leave it right there and to convince oneself that it looks really perfect in that spot.

I digress, but it is summer and the use of the name "playroom" still represents a kind of personal rebellion on my part, I think. Today people have "great rooms". Ours is great but is not a "great room". Previously people had "family rooms". Ours has always been used by the family but is not and has never been a "family room". Some have called similar rooms the "TV room" and while there has always been a TV in that room it has never been the "TV room". It is and will continue to be the "playroom" containing the original toy chest, albeit refinished to look like the mahogany, but still filled by that assortment of broken and fun toys that the grandchildren love.

We had a house girl, everyone did, forty pesos a month. She lived in. All the houses had separate rooms for the help. She was young and sweet and learned whatever you taught her including using indoor plumbing which was strange and new to her. In spite of our having a washing machine she preferred to wash the clothes by hand outside in a small square concrete open enclosure. She would beat the clothes on the cement which was the local custom, effective for stain removal, but very hard on the clothes.

She loved children and so was a wonderful babysitter. (Isn't it strange how every young mother says the same thing about every babysitter or nanny?)

But I don't want you to get the wrong idea when I say it was like a fancy federal prison - it was. Actually we could go into the local town, but it was so dirty and so strange to our "Ugly American" sensibilities that we stuck close to the base and to home. We were discouraged from traveling to Manila both by the Air Force and by the rigors of the trip and most especially by the thought of leaving the children in the care of strangers if something happened to us. So many prisons are of our own making.

On base we could go to the PX and the Officers' Club and the movies; the only three places that were air conditioned. The movie air lasted about twenty minutes so it was the PX or the Club. The PX had food and gifty kind of things, clothing and brass candlesticks and velvet paintings (tackiest) and beautiful embroidered linens and barong Tagalog's which the local men wore for dress and which would today be smashing as women's jackets. But what did we know? Practically nothing.

While I call it a kind of prison, it really afforded me a great deal of freedom. The house girl would stay with Steven, the baby, and I could take Little Larry and Kevin, then two and a half and one and a half to the pool every day. It was quite lovely, surrounded by poinsettia bushes which grew to about twenty feet and by Christmas were covered with blooms which made beautiful arrangements so long as one burned the cut ends to staunch the heavy white sap.

Being in the service meant lots of social invitations. We had spent four years of med school and one of internship as social hermits of necessity. It was fun to be able to entertain and to be entertained.

At the age of 24, I learned to swim. My childhood summers had been spent at the Jersey Shore where the surf was wonderfully rough, but learning to swim was impossible. One can't stand in a pool for too long, however, without looking and feeling pretty foolish so I signed up for the Red

Cross lessons and finished up to Life Saving at which time I was pregnant again and the idea of having to lift the lifeguard stand from the deep end of the pool was inadvisable. All of the kids learned to swim early and well and I learned to enjoy their water achievements as I had not had the time to enjoy their first steps. While life there was very constricted it was pleasant.

After several months, I had a miscarriage - a sad and strange experience. I delivered a fetus that was almost fully formed and Larry baptized it. Boy or girl? I don't know. Was their time for me to grieve? No, not really. It was something we kept to ourselves in those days. And then a minor problem requiring a DNC, no big deal medically. So off we went to the Base Hospital which was just a cluster of Quonset huts connected by covered walkways. It was the rainy season so as they rolled me on the gurney from my room to the operating room, the rain fell on me. It was as though God were giving me a blessing with cool holy water.

In the OR there was lots of social banter; remember this was a simple DNC and I knew all the doctors socially. They put an IV into my arm and suddenly I was paralyzed. I could not move anything but my eyes and the last digit of my fingers. I could not cry out. But most important I could not take another breath and as the last one went out and my chest tightened, I went unconscious. I woke up back in my room where Larry was waiting. I started yelling, "They tried to kill me!" My husband was a wonderful family practitioner partly because he was a doctor who listened, who stayed calm. (Sometimes to the point of extreme.)

He tried to calm me down and quite frankly was acting as though I was crazy. I was ranting, raving actually, which was not my usual mode but it had been an incredibly scary experience and he didn't seem to believe me.

And in walked the anesthesiologist. I don't remember his name, but I will always remember his hang dog look. "I am so sorry, Mary."

"What did you do to me? You almost killed me!"

"Oh no. The tube to the IV had not been changed from the previous abdominal surgery where we used curare after the patient was intubated. So you received a few drops of curare by mistake, but we knew right away what had happened."

"Oh, really?" I knew from those last few seconds that no one knew anything right away. I couldn't move or speak or breathe my next breath but I could see and hear and they didn't know anything right away.

It took a long time for me to get over my near death experience. A friend of ours who was a priest used to come for dinner occasionally. I told him I was really troubled by the experience and he probed gently, "Why? What about it is so upsetting?"

I thought for a few minutes and finally told him that in those, what I believed to be my final moments, all I could think about was how angry I was with the doctor's stupidity, no thought of God, no life flashing before my eyes, no thought of my love or my babies.

The priest was quiet for a long time. He looked into my eyes and said, "Mary, were you ready to die at that moment?"

There was a long pause on my part. "I guess I was as ready as I'll ever be."

"So then stop worrying," he said. "We die the way we live."

He was a wise man and a good priest. His advice has stayed with me ever since.

Prison Break

IT WAS SPRINGTIME AND IN THE PHILIPPINES THAT MEANT
HOT, HOTTER, HOTTEST! We had made many friends,
but there were two couples in particular that we saw
frequently often to play bridge with. They were our
kind of bridge players, beginners like us and not
adverse to a little cheating, signals, a certain knee
tap under the table or raising of an eyebrow, stuff
like that which was lots of fun. In the service there
are an awful lot of really serious bridge players who
would lie when you say 'oh we are just beginners'
and they reply 'oh, so are we'. But an evening with
these people turns into torture. So we got to be
very careful in choosing bridge partners.

These were fun friends. One was a psychiatrist
and his wife, Dianne. The other was the hospital
administrator and his wife also Diane. The second Diane was from Minnesota and was the only
person of all the people we met there who had a
mom or anyone who actually came to visit.

In preparation for her mother's visit, Diane
decided that it would be fun to take her mom to
Hong Kong. There were arrangements that could
be made for them to travel "space available".
There were always flights going back and forth

to Hong Kong and Air Force dependents could always hitch a ride.

Quickly it was decided that we, the other Dianne and I, would go with them. It would be like a real vacation, a break from the base, what I have called the Prison, a kind of prison break.

I was about seven months pregnant with John, but the OB Doctor saw no problem with me going. It was a short trip by air and it would be fun. A real city, shops, restaurants, sights to be seen! How exciting!

And so we went. My fear of flying was stifled by the thought of such a real vacation. I don't know which one of us decided on the hotel, but, of course, we didn't want to splurge on that when there was so much else to spend our funds on. So the place where we stayed was inexpensive, so inexpensive that all night the doors on the hall were opening and closing. We realized in the morning that with lots of servicemen around the area we were probably in a kind of brothel.

But let me tell you about Diane's mom. We all listen to the radio show on NPR, Garrison Keeler, and his description of Minnesota, where all the women are strong, the men good looking and the children above average. And when he speaks about Minnesota and the adversity of the weather and the strength of the folks, well when we met Diane's mom, we met one of the folks he talks about. She was fun, charming, and really strong. She could walk and walk and walk and not be tired. No afternoon naps for her.

I remember one afternoon when we had pretty much exhausted our shopping budgets, it was decided that we would go to the Tiger Balm Gardens, a kind of Botanical Garden in the heart of the City. The hills and paths quickly wore me out and I sat down on a bench looking out at the beautiful garden and they agreed to pick me up there a little later. Larry had sent me with a new camera with instructions to take lots of pictures for him. So I sat on that bench and aimed the camera this way and that, not being particularly adept or even interested in the finished product.

After a few minutes, a man approached me and told me that I should not take pictures into the sun. He had such a heavy, thick drawl that it took me a few minutes to begin to understand him, I think he was from Texas and I, trying not to hurt his feelings, complied with his directions as best as I could, thanked him and he walked on. Those pictures were really terrible.

Shortly after my Texan encounter I, being pregnant needed a restroom. There it was right on the path. It had two swinging doors, chin to knee high like barroom doors in cowboy movies, and behind which was a hole in the ground with two foot prints one on each side. The hole wasn't so bad, well that's not really true, but compared to those doors it wasn't. The people passing by the swinging doors whose heads and shoulders were visible, that was the bad part. I think I went in and out and in and out many times before I realized that it was all that there was and I had to ignore the passersby.

The ladies returned and that night we celebrated our last night in Hong Kong by having dinner at a fancy hotel restaurant on a hill overlooking the harbor. It was a magnificent sight as the darkness fell and the lights of the sampans and the cruise ships lit the scene below. My psychiatrist Dianne was a Southern belle who insisted that she would start with the oysters. I never knew a person who ate oysters and we all thought it would be fun to watch her eat them, no chewing, just swallow was the proper form, and she did.

We had lots of fun that night. The food was great and the sights remarkable. Of course, we had lots of wine since it was not safe to drink the water. We had been warned: don't drink the water; don't brush your teeth in the water; don't drink anything that had ice cubes in it. But the city of Hong Kong was so clean. It consisted of two parts, one half on the mainland of China and the other half on an island, connected by ferry service that was fast and reliable and clean. The stairs up and down to the boats clean and clear of litter, so unlike public transport in New York City. But the water, we had to watch the water.

We thought that we had complied with the water restrictions, but that night Dianne and I, who were sharing a room, were terribly sick. Something vile and awful had gotten us and as we tried to pack for the trip back "home" we were really dragging, wondering how we would make it to the plane and the ride back to Clark.

How strange to think of it now, to call Clark Air Force Base, "home". What a many layered term, "home "is; what does it mean? Comfort, security, safety, love, family, my own bed so important when one is sick and my own doctor to take care of me and to cure me; all wrapped in that lovely word, "home".

Clark Air Force Base was the largest Air Base in the world in 1961, it was a SAC Base, a Strategic Air Command Field where big bombers took off and landed every day, all day and all night. They were a kind of standing flying army. It was the Cold War. Only recently did my husband tell me of his thoughts each time he would race with the ambulances and rescue trucks to the flight line on word that a bomber was in trouble; how he thought what an exercise in futility it all would be in the event of a real crash since the bellies of those monster planes held atomic bombs.

Kids back home in the U.S .were learning to hide under desks at school; almost as silly as ambulances to the flight line in case of a crash. We were really in a state of readiness for war with Russia and that war would be atomic. As Air Force dependents we had been notified to draft an inventory of all our household goods and their value and to have a get up and go bag, one for each of us, adults and children, in case of an emergency evacuation. The lurking danger we all learned to ignore. We didn't even really talk about it. It was home and the prison break was over.

Insiders Outside

SOMETIME IN EARLY 1960, LARRY GOT ORDERS TO SERVE TEMPORARY DUTY AT THE CLINIC IN BAGUIO, BUT THIS TIME WE WERE ALL TO GO WITH HIM FOR THE TWO WEEKS. Baguio was located in the mountains, it was beautiful and lush, orchids grew in wild profusion by the side of the roads, the sun shone brightly all day, but nights were wonderfully cool, cool enough for us to try to start a fire in the fireplace but the wood was wet and the only paper available was toilet paper. We came dangerously close to running out in our futile attempts to have a fire one night.

Our house girl, Belin, had come with us and one afternoon she suggested that we might want to go downtown to the market place, an open bazaar to shop. Fruits, vegetables, meats, trinkets, clothing, it was a veritable department store under tents in a large square. My boys, then three, two and one were particularly intrigued by the Negrito men who were short and slender, very dark skinned with wiry kinky hair. They wore loin cloths and leather Air Force Bomber jackets. As we stood in the square, Kevin, the two year old, couldn't resist trying to pinch the bare bottom of one of the men. I scolded firmly, but the Negrito only laughed and called out to his friends. Before long, there was a crowd gathering around us. Belin had gone off to shop and my husband was wandering. As the crowd grew and the men started to touch my babies stroking their hair and feeling their noses and pointing to their eyes, suddenly out of the Tagalog jumble, I heard one shout "Ten centavos to see these children."

The apologetic smile that I had pasted on my face at the beginning started to dissolve. Fear in the belly! My babies were freaks to these mountain men. Their red hair, white skin, blue eyes and thin noses were as strange to them as their attire and stature were to us. And then Belin came running, screaming at the crowd and chased them off.

"Oh, Mrs, I'm so sorry. I shouldn't have left you. They mean no harm." And of course, I knew that, but the fleeting fear haunted me.

We were the real outsiders in that country. On a personal level we didn't want to be there. In truth, politically we were occupiers and had been for a very long time. Most of the time the Filipinos with whom we dealt made us feel very welcome. We were the employers bringing dollars and prosperity to the few. But the country as a whole was terribly poor. The infrastructure was corrupt. One had to bribe the local official if one needed to get something signed and give the man at the desk another bribe to bring the papers into the next fellow inside for him to sign. Understandably there was an underlying hostility to Americans. The United States had been there for many years. American servicemen had liberated the country in the Second World War, but not before the people had suffered long and mightily at the hands of the Japanese.

Inside out or outside in? Who decides?

John Francis and Donna

MY FOURTH SON, JOHN FRANCIS, WAS BORN IN THE HOS-
PITAL ON CLARK AIR FORCE BASE IN THE PHILIPPINE
ISLANDS ON MAY 25, 1960, BEARING DUAL CITIZENSHIP WHICH
WAS THE BANE OF HIS EXISTENCE AS A YOUNGSTER SUBJECTED
TO THE TEASING OF HIS THREE OLDER BROTHERS THAT HE
WAS "A FILIPINO". His labor and delivery were the easi-
est of all my children and his infancy was wonderfully
relaxed. Every new mother should have full time help
especially when there are three older boys all under
four.

By the end of that June we realized that the
Air Force, in true Service tradition, had miscalcu-
lated our time owed. To our undying gratitude,
they told us we owed one more year instead of
four. Delighted we looked forward to our next
assignment. With Larry's accumulated leave time
it would only be six months of active duty. We
were now a full household: four babies, lots of furniture and much stuff. They had to send us someplace close to home. It would not be reasonable
to do otherwise. So we waited with anticipation
but not apprehension. Surely they wouldn't send
us to someplace like Alaska, not after the Philippines, and not for just six months.

One bright sunny morning (they were all bright and sunny except in the rainy season when they all were wet and bleak) my husband called from the clinic on base. "We got our orders, dear."

"Oh, where are they sending us now?" Assured that nothing could be as bad as that first set of orders, I was cheerfully anticipating the next step.

"We are going to Albany," he said.

"Albany! Why would they send us all the way up to Albany?" I asked incredulous at the incompetence of his employer.

"No Dear, we are not going up to Albany, we are going down to Albany. Albany, Georgia."

And so in September of that year starting his two month leave, we flew home to New York. My sister had suggested that instead of trying to squeeze into my mom's and then Larry's mom's houses, we rent a house in Rockaway Point. It was after Labor Day and houses were available and not too expensive. It was a great idea! It was close to family in Bay Ridge and Woodhaven for visits. She took care of the details and the thought of two months on the beach took a little of the edge from our trip "down" to Georgia.

The house was a substantial one, a two story house with a raised foundation. One morning about two weeks after we had moved in, when the baby started to cry, my husband offered to get up with him and let me sleep. Quickly he came back and woke me with the news that the radio was talking about a hurricane and that maybe we should take everybody into his mom's in Woodhaven just to be safe.

At that instant I became aware of the sound of the wind and the rain against the house which was really just a bungalow, it was a pounding sound almost a feeling that the house was shaking. Quickly we dressed and put a few things in a bag and hurried to get off the island. By the time we reached the bridge the water was up to the top of the hubcaps. It was a real Hurricane with a name that I now know to be "Donna". But we could not return to the house for a couple of weeks. When we did the house was still standing relatively undamaged, but the houses around it were either gone or demolished as though some flat footed monster had walked the various walks that constituted Rockaway Point leaving incredible damage behind. Then we had to wait another few days for the water to be connected before we were allowed to return.

As we inched toward our departure date of November 1st, Georgia looked better and better. Rockaway was desolate and so very sad after that storm.

And so onto the next chapter.

Marching To Georgia

Larry had to go to Turner Air Force Base, in Georgia that November, to find a house for us. He did, 47 Force Drive, Albany, Georgia. The babies and I were to follow soon after by train into Atlanta where he would pick us up and drive the rest of the way to Albany located in the southwestern corner of Georgia. My father-in-law drove us to New York Grand Central Station where he helped us to get on board and settled. I had chosen the last car in the hope that there would not be so many people and that the kids would have more space to play and spread out. It seemed a good choice because the car was almost empty.

Around 4:30 the conductor came through to announce the first seating for dinner and I quickly figured that would be our best bet. I gathered everyone together, baby in arms and as we approached the doors between the speeding cars I realized the error of my choice. There was no way I could carry the baby and hold the hands of even one of the three boys and open the two doors and jump over that speeding gap. I certainly couldn't take one of them at a time because they would never just stay put on the other side and what about the baby? I couldn't leave him on a seat as I managed the others. With the vision of a night without supper, I was close to tears.

And then an elderly couple (probably fiftyish) approached and asked if we were going to the four thirty supper seating. Laughing, I said "I was trying, but I don't see how that's going to happen."

"Oh, we'll be happy to help you," they said. And so they did, taking one of the boys at a time across the "abyss" and then repeating the process several times until we reached the dining car many cars away. They sat close by and told me that when we were finished they would help us back. There are moments in life when you can't help but believe in God and know that She really is watching over you.

The next morning we arrived in Atlanta and there was Larry waiting for us. What a welcome sight! It was only five more hours in the car before we reached our new house. Thank God there was no rule then about babies under five being secured in car seats.

Albany, Georgia in the Fall and Spring of '60-'61 was a place that felt like another country, another year, another time, more foreign in many ways than the Philippines: Public Water fountains marked "Whites Only", balcony seats in the movie house marked "Colored", a big Catholic Church and Catholic School for Whites and a separate run down Church and School for the Blacks.

One day I went to the butcher shop where I stood on line waiting my turn. There were three people in front of me all of whom happened to be black. The butcher was white. He looked up from what he was doing and as soon as he saw me, he smiled and said, "Can I help you?"

I thought it was strange and as I looked at the people in front of me I said, "I'll wait my turn. These folks are ahead of me." It was perfectly plain that they were ahead of me. It didn't need saying.

"Madam, may I help you?" There was an edge in his voice which now was a little louder: an implicit command that implied that the people in front of me were invisible somehow. The butcher was clearly annoyed. Could he detect my New York accent perhaps?

"No, thank you. I'll wait," I said in my most indignant tone.

The three people in front of me never looked up, didn't say a word, but turned and left the store and I did likewise. But this was Albany, Georgia, and the reason this incident stays in my memory so clearly is that in a few short months Albany, Georgia, was the birthplace of the Civil Rights Movement. How did people who had been treated like dirt for so long, who had caved in without a word so many times, do what they did? I don't know.

When we subsequently moved to Smithtown, New York, where my husband set up private practice as a Family Doctor, I got involved in local political action in response to the assassinations of President John F. Kennedy and Dr. Martin Luther King. Some of the ordinary people of my town decided that the only way that we could somehow make our voices heard in the face of the incredible national turmoil that was enveloping the country, was to lobby for a local Open Housing Ordinance, (Smithtown was 99.99% White and we knew that didn't just happen). It was really along the line of a "drop in the bucket" sort of thing. But it quickly escalated from speaking at Town Board Meetings to a planned march down Main Street on a Saturday morning, children in tow, placards and all. Oh, we were a scraggly bunch!

There I was, with my three boys and my baby in the stroller and the thought that I was probably not really helping my husband's fledging medical practice, but no matter how I tried I could not get out of my mind those people in Albany, Georgia, the folks in that butcher shop, the police dogs, the water cannons, the beatings. When people spat on me and my babies in my own new hometown and shouted obscenities, I was frightened and repulsed but also just a little bit proud.

A Terrible Thief

AFTER A WHIRLWIND PREGNANCY: MOVING FROM GEORGIA, FINDING A PRACTICE, A NEW HOUSE, GETTING SETTLED, CURTAINS, FURNITURE AND ALL THAT, ON AUGUST 18TH 1961, LATE IN THE DAY I WENT INTO LABOR AND AFTER A QUICK VISIT TO THE DOCTOR, LARRY AND I ALMOST FLEW DOWN TO GOOD SAMARITAN HOSPITAL IN BAY SHORE SINCE SMITHTOWN GENERAL WAS NOT YET OPEN. This was number five. Things were moving very fast.

During the last several months of this pregnancy while we were staying with Mrs. Werner, Larry's mom, in Woodhaven, I had made a special effort to see the obstetrician in Smithtown so that we could get to know each other. I had assured him I was healthy as a horse, I was not a screamer and that I wanted to be awake for my delivery as I had been for the other four. I was an early advocate of Dr. Grantly Dick Reid's Natural Childbirth. He had assured me that he was marking my chart to that effect and that I was not to worry about it. Each time I trucked out to see him I mentioned it again just to be sure since the usual practice at that time was to put the mom to sleep.

Good Sam's Admission Office quickly realized the urgency of my condition and hustled me to the Delivery Room where the doctor met me and after a brief exam suddenly gave me a shot before I could ask, "What is that?" and that was the last thing I knew.

I awoke at three o'clock in the morning, in a darkened room, clearly without my pregnant belly. My body was still half asleep, but my mind was racing. Something's wrong! Something had to be wrong! Why else would this doctor put me to sleep when the delivery was just a few minutes away? And I had told him repeatedly that I wanted to be awake. I quickly rang for the nurse.

"What went wrong with my baby?" I said.

"Oh nothing, you have a beautiful baby girl."

"I want to see her".

"Dear, you can't see her now. Go to sleep. It's three o'clock in the morning."

I was terrified, sure that something awful had happened. When the nurse left me I was still groggy from the drugs and couldn't get up. I think I would have run down the hall to the nursery if I could have. Instead, I called my husband demanding to know what was wrong with the baby. He was sound sleep and for a few minutes he couldn't figure out what I was talking about.

"What do you mean? Everything is fine," he said.

But it wasn't! That moment of awesome transformation, of birth, of miracle had been taken, robbed by this beast of a doctor! How I hated what he had done! How unforgivable! How very masculine! He decided to take from me my life giving, God sharing experience without even a thought. Without a by your leave!

There are many moments that I look back on in my life that contributed to the making of this feminist and this was one of them. How dare he?

Maryann was not only all right but a sweet and happy baby (maybe it was the drugs) who has grown into a wonderful, very competent woman albeit not too sentimental about family pianos.

Many wrongs in life are, over the course of time, woven and buried into the warp and woof of living, gently forgiven if not forgotten. But as fate would have it this pregnancy and birth would be my last that could be fairly called normal, the last time that I could have had that ever so special moment and so there has been no forgetting and even less forgiving.

This thief took something of great value!

The Phlox

IT WAS A BEAUTIFUL SHINING DAY. The sun was bright and hot. The sky was Carolina blue. It was late June, the 25th, 1963, and our brand new bluestone patio had just been finished. It was beautiful, but more than a little bare around the edges. So off to the nursery I went and returned with flats of perennial phlox. It was pretty much all they had left. They looked more than a little sad, since it was late June and way past the prime planting season. I quickly changed into my big maternity bathing suit and gathered a comfortable pillow, a big sun hat and a spade and set to work with the hose at the ready to cool me off and to water the new plantings.

That evening I had an appointment with my new OB doctors, Dr. Zuckerman, a mercurial kind of guy who thought nothing of yelling at his patients if the scale showed an extra pound, and Dr. Schiffman, a calm Southern gentleman from Texas. By that time Larry had been in practice in Smithtown a couple of years and had gotten to know these two doctors and he recommended them highly. And besides, their waiting room had on one wall a huge mural of a beautiful very pregnant young woman in profile that made all the pregnant moms feel eminently petite and their dressing rooms had beaded curtains instead of the usual hospital canvas. In other words they were "with it" and I had no fear that they would not respect my wishes.

That night my appointment was with Dr. Zuckerman, the yeller. He took one look at my chart and started.

"You haven't had your blood test!" he said. No actually he really shouted it. "Go NOW to the hospital and have it done, tonight, and come back here with the results. If the titers are up we really want to think about inducing this baby."

Erythroblastosis is an onomatopoeia word. It sounds as ugly and destructive as it is. It is the condition of the mom's blood destroying the baby's blood. Instead of nourishing that little life in the womb, the mom is unwittingly and uncontrollably killing it.

We had known from the beginning that Larry and I were incompatible, blood wise from the Rh point of view. God knows we were compatible in every other way! But I was positive and he was negative. However, he was heterozygous which meant kind of not so bad and besides we already had five babies who were not affected so I had developed the attitude of the young. It can never happen to me, but that wonderful impatient doctor knew better. He knew the chance I was taking by not keeping on top of the blood titer test. They were just starting at that time to do intrauterine transfusions. So he insisted. I went. And he was right.

When I returned to his office with the results, the titers were considerably raised and after a thorough examination he thought the baby big enough to try to deliver him early. He hoped I would go into labor naturally. That night I did and the next morning off we went to the hospital.

I don't remember whether I was actually in the Delivery Room, but I knew I was close and suddenly labor stopped. There is an aura when something is wrong. Everyone started running. Larry bent to my ear and quietly said that the baby had turned in the birth canal and they would have to do a caesarean section quickly to get him out. I would have a spinal and would be awake and I should not worry that everything would be okay. He was so calm he calmed me, almost.

Things moved quickly, so quickly that I actually felt the incision, not in a painful way but almost like a feather running down my abdomen. But that baby was really wedged in the birth canal. Dr. Zuckerman was soon cursing and Dr. Schiffman was shouting commands and the table was actually shaking under me and for the first time I really didn't want to be awake for this delivery.

The anesthesiologist was whispering in my ear, "Don't get sick. Swallow. Breathe."

And then the magic words, "It's a boy."

"Thank you God."

But wait - there was no cry. There was much activity on the other side of the room around the bassinet. But no cry. "Oh God, please let him cry." And then he did cry.

They had suctioned him and slapped him progressively harder and finally he cried and after they cleaned him up they showed him very briefly to me and whisked him off to the preemie nursery where they started an exchange transfusion, dripping his blood out one heel and infusing new blood in the other. He had three of these transfusions in the next several days and then started to thrive. Meanwhile, I was getting from Demerol shot to Demerol shot almost not caring about anything but the pain. That pulling and tugging had done some job on my intestines.

The preemie nurses kept bothering me that they needed a name for this sick baby. It helps them to talk to the babies in the incubators if they have a name. He was so early we hadn't even talked about a name. So I told Larry, "Go home and ask the boys what they want to name their new baby brother."

He returned with the logical choice. It was the week that Pope Paul the Sixth was named pope so the boys, having had more than their usual dose of TV, logically decided that number six should be Paul. And so it was.

Paul stayed in the hospital for several weeks and I went home after two. The day I left, Dr. Zuckerman came in to give me all the usual instructions but added two that were definitely different, "You can't do anything for eight weeks, I mean nothing and no more babies. Your uterus won't take it."

"You're kidding aren't you?" I said.

"Don't tell me your social problems. Just do what you are told. And you will be okay."

Again he was right. I couldn't do anything for about eight weeks. My mother and father stayed with me and were wonderful and I lay on that new patio and marveled at the phlox. My father was a city gardener. He figured if he diddled the soil, pulled any intruding weeds and watered and watered and watered things would grow. They did. The phlox were tall and white and in bloom when I arrived home and continued for the whole summer. The fragrance was fabulous. The baby was good.

Those same phlox are still in my garden. I've moved them. I've divided them. I've given them away.

And that baby, Paul, is a handsome lawyer and the father of three beautiful girls. His years between that day and this would fill three volumes, but I don't think I can write those volumes. Some things you can't write. I keep giving him some of his phlox, but he is not as successful as his grandfather was but I will keep on trying. His wife, Susan recently called to tell us to hold the date, May 14th, 2011 for the girls B'not Mitzvah. The oldest two are twins. And we are saving January 31st, 2015 for their youngest's Bat Mitzvah

L'chaim!

Margaret

OVER THE YEARS PEOPLE HAVE ASKED US WHY WE HAD SO MANY CHILDREN. We never thought of them as "so many", but as I have started to look back on my life for the purpose of writing my memoirs the question has occurred to me as well.

The easy answer is we were and remain Catholics and everyone knows the Catholic position on birth control. But, while we were both brought up Catholic the question of birth control never entered our vocabulary, (same as sex actually) until we were well into our married life and had already had several children.

Love to us was and is procreative: a little like the gardener who can't stand to see a new plant and not take a cutting and try to make it grow. To use an earthy metaphor, sex was and is like the glue that holds marriages together and the fertilizer that makes real love grow. So sex by the calendar was impossible and those rubbery things were simply unacceptable and the pills were medically contraindicated. And besides, there was that "increase and multiply" thing. We always wanted a big family. We wanted lots of children. Well, maybe not so close together but these things do happen.

Then came the "yelling Doctor" and the "no more baby's speech". After Paul's birth and the long convalescence it involved, the thought of another baby became how to say it, more dangerous. Rhythm in music may be great but in sex it is ridiculous.

And so, I became pregnant again. There ensued days of regrets and worries about what I had done. For the first time I think I had actually decided that I would have this one more baby. The others had just happened in the normal course of events.

I had a friend who was a wonderful seamstress who actually designed her own clothes. She had an incredible sense of fashion and so as soon as she decided to have her last baby, at about the same time as I was pregnant, she got to work on her maternity wardrobe. I got to work thinking and praying over the foolishness of what I had done.

At about three months, while I was still not hardly showing she was so big she could no longer fit into her beautiful maternity clothes and she magnanimously gifted me with her most fashionable wardrobe. She subsequently delivered two full term seven pound boys. But I mention this because she gave me such a lift, at a time when I was depressed and very much worried about the wrongheadedness of my decision. I don't like to admit to such vanity but when one is down and worried, looking fabulous doesn't hurt.

One morning late in September of 1965, I was about six and one half months along. I awoke with a terrible, constant pain. My belly was hard as a rock. No Braxton-Hicks these! I woke Larry who remained calm until the blood started. Hemorrhage is another of those onomatopoeia words.

Immediately he got the OB Doctor on the phone and came back to the bedroom and said, "We have to go to the hospital right away. Get dressed." To this day he denies ever telling me to get dressed, but I remember thinking that he didn't understand how I was feeling. "Get dressed". What a ridiculous idea. And yet I did, and off to the hospital we went.

This time as I lay totally naked on the operating table and the doctors who now included pediatricians and nurses and others rushed around me, there was no desire to be awake. All I could think of was please cover my nakedness and please put me to sleep.

Another spinal was given; no trouble getting this tiny little baby out, as well as all the baby producing parts which had ruptured; no cries heard; a girl, baptized quickly as she was whisked to the preemie nursery where new blood was to be given. It was much later that I learned that the hospital only had one unit of the appropriate blood and that they gave it to me. One of the OR nurses actually gave our baby live blood.

We named her Margaret Alice. My middle name and my father's younger sister's name was Margaret and my mother was Alice. I had never liked the name of Alice but by this time in my life I had developed an appreciation of and for my mother and wanted to honor her in this way. We did not know if the baby would survive. I healed quickly and learned how much easier it is to recover from removing innards than it is from repairing them.

They say they gave her five complete transfusions, but I really believe that they just kept on giving her new blood and taking out her diseased blood. She was in the hospital for two months and came home just about the time she would have been due to be born but by then she was barely five pounds.

She was still in the hospital during the '65 blackout and when Larry called his service that night to tell them that he would call them every half hour because our phones were hooked up electrically and weren't ringing, I remember the feeling of disaster when the service operator told him, "Oh Doctor Werner, the lights are out all over Long Island, all over the Eastern Seaboard, out in Canada; something terrible has happened."

After being assured that the hospital generators were up and working and that Margaret was fine, we went on eating our supper, but the unspoken fear was there, was this to be our last meal, was this some kind of nuclear accident or even worse an attack by Russia? Thank God, we didn't have a president who immediately thought of retribution without even knowing against whom to retribute. Life went on. A mere accident, electrical domino effect, they said.

But then came the search for what damage Margaret had suffered, not from any blackout but from the erythroblastosis. What had this done to her? She was an adorable handful, a red haired, happy baby. All she seemed to want to do was to sleep and the only thing I had to do was to wake her every half hour to feed her. Life has a way of playing jokes on us. I had had two non-sleepers and now I had a sleeper who refused to wake up. We would stroke her little feet, tickle her, shake her a little, all to no avail. If she took a half an ounce, we would celebrate.

And we watched her. Could she have survived all that without real damage? She followed us with her eyes when they were open and soon started to react to us. She made the usual baby noises. Even when she woke in the night she didn't cry but rather babbled. Surely a good sign! I used to change the babies on the kitchen table and I would knock on the table and she would turn. Her hearing seemed to be ok. She was very slow to sit up, but Larry assured me that for preemies like her, it usually took two years for them to catch up.

Then Larry's mom got sick, a stroke, I think. She needed nursing care and his father, wonderful guy that he was, was not up to this particular job and so when Larry realized that help was needed he called me one Wednesday when he was in visiting and said, "I think I need to bring my mother home." and of course I said, "Fine." Funny, we never thought of hiring someone. Money was not plentiful and although people thought the Doctor must be rich it was never so. But he came from a family of seven and instead of them volunteering to help, all they did was come to our house to visit Mom so on top of taking care of Mrs. Werner (I never could call her anything else) I had all this extra company. Finally I wised up and told them that when they came they could watch my two babies and I would go out and shop (or do nothing). Eventually, the visits slowed down.

One morning, after I had cleaned up Mrs. Werner and changed her and the bed and washed her and combed her long hair and rolled it as best I could into the bun she wore, I then went down the hall to Margaret who had a little cold and was whinging in her crib at the other end of the house. Not crying, just not happy. As I approached the door I was doing the "Okay Margaret, I'm here, it's okay." As I entered her room and stood in the doorway, she was standing in her crib, looking out the window and suddenly I realized, SHE CAN'T HEAR ME.

All those months of searching for whatever damage her birth had caused - neurological, visual, and mental, it was almost a relief. She can't hear. I can deal with that. I thought. But I had no idea what that meant, I didn't know the years of learning for me as well as for her that it entailed. And when Larry came home for lunch that day he said he knew but figured there was nothing we could do yet anyway so he decided it would be better if I discovered it on my own.

I have told Margie many times, she taught me that I could do anything.

FAMILY PHOTO (1968) FROM BACK ROW, L. TO R. - KEVIN, LARRY, STEVEN, MARYANN, JOHN, PAUL, MARGARET

Testing 1, 2, 3

LARRY HAD A PATIENT WHO HAD THREE SONS WHO HAD BEEN BORN DEAF AND HE ADVISED US NOT TO SUBJECT MARGARET TO THE TORTURE OF ENDLESS TRIPS TO DIFFERENT SPECIALISTS. They recommended Long Island Jewish Hearing and Speech as the best in the area and so we went. Actually we didn't go, I went with Margaret.

The first step after an interview with the audiologist was to determine whether she had any hearing at all. So we sat in the sound proof booth. She comfortably ensconced on my lap with a toy I grew to hate in her hands while the audiologist looking through a large window watched Margaret very closely for any sign of hearing, a look, a turn of the head, while she piped in sounds first from the left speaker then the right speaker. These were what are called pure sounds. As they kept coming with no reaction from my baby, I started to get frantic. The audiologist's voice was studied and calm, reassuring me that there was nothing to worry about. Beep, nothing; beep, nothing; louder, louder, louder until I was barely able to stand it. It was hurting my ears. And then suddenly Margaret, for a short moment, looked at the corner of the room from where the sound was coming.

"She heard that," the audiologist said. "I think that is enough for today".

As we went outside I was full of questions. "What is the level of her hearing?" I asked.

She hemmed and hawed a little bit, but finally said, "Well, if she were standing beside a huge jumbo jet and all of its engines were running full throttle, she might just hear something."

"When can we fit her with a hearing aid?" I just wanted to fix this problem as soon and as fast as possible. "Do they make aids that powerful?" I thought that was the answer. People who were hard of hearing wore hearing aids and they heard.

"Mrs. Werner, You don't understand." she said. "We can't amplify sound for Margaret until we have a good hearing test. We don't want to hurt what little hearing she has. So we will have to teach her to tell us when she hears."

That's where that infernal toy came in. Every parent of a child has seen one and probably played with one. It's a white post with different colored circles, doughnut-like rings that fit on the post eventually in size order. LIJ used it to train a child to hold the ring to her ear and put it on the post when she heard anything. Sounds simple huh? But Margaret couldn't hear. But she was smart and she knew we wanted her to put those rings on that post and so she did. Of course we knew it was not a sign of her hearing anything, she just wanted to please us.

So week after week we went back, at first back to the testing room, the silent room, and then to spend an hour with an audiologist who tried to show me how to teach my daughter how to read my lips and to speak and to put those rings on that post but only when she heard something. All the while never giving me a direct answer to my repeated questions, "What can I expect of this baby?"

Postscript: this baby is today a successful Social Worker!

Miracles in all Forms

WE WENT EVERY WEEK. Every week I asked, "What can I expect of this child?" "What should I be doing?"

Their answer was that I should expose her to sound, as much sound as possible. So we bought a very powerful Hi-fi and headphones and Margaret and I sat at the dining room table while I turned the volume louder and louder, until I suspected that she was hearing something.

I remember a particular record I used. It was the Medical Missionary Sisters singing sweet gospel-like songs. What a silly choice. I should have gotten a deep baritone singing "Old Man River" or something like that, but what did I know? The song I remember was "Zacheas Come Down". It was the gospel story about a little guy who was too short to see Jesus in the crowds so he climbed a tree and of course, Jesus saw him and told him to come down and that he would dine with him that very night. I think the appeal of that rather silly song was that I felt so far down and was waiting in my own way for Jesus to invite me to dinner, but the invitation was not forthcoming. But maybe, if I am to be honest, it did come, albeit in a different form.

I found the John Tracy Clinic, a free corre-spondence course meant to help the moms of deaf babies and young children. I can't remem-ber whether the Clinic at Long Island Jewish Medical Center (LIJ) recommended it or I just somehow found it. After filling out and sending a kind of information sheet, within a few days they sent me the first lesson. A couple of pages of wonderful, specific instructions and techniques to help me to teach her, then a page on which I could write my comments or questions and the very next week, the next lesson would come and all my questions and more would be answered, hand written.

John Tracy was born in 1925, the son of Spen-cer Tracy and Louise Treadwell Tracy. He was diagnosed as profoundly deaf. His mother taught him to speak and to lip read. His father was a suc-cessful movie star who carried on a rather pub-lic affair with Katherine Hepburn for about forty years. He was such a "good Catholic" that he would never get a divorce.

In 1945, Louise Treadmill Tracy got together with ten other mothers of deaf babies and decided that they needed to do something to help each other and others and so was founded the John Tracy Clinic. Free. I suppose that Spencer's money was responsible, but that is just conjecture on my part. Whatever pain and humiliation she suffered as a result of his rather public liaison, she did great good with her life.

The John Tracy Clinic is still in existence and has helped over 100,000 babies and moms. So many times good comes from evil, most times we don't realize it or even think about it until much later.

And then the learning started. First step was to get Margaret's attention. She was just two. Stroke her cheek gently until she looks up. Then say the word, one word, and try to have the object in your hand close to your mouth at the same time so she makes the connection. Over and over and over again. Then we graduated to having her feel my lips when she looked. Put her hand on my throat to feel vibrations. Feel the sound of "B" buh, ball buh. The slight rush of air through the lips. Ah but so many sounds, so many words look the same, feel the same. I don't know how long it was before she said "ball" or what was to me a wonderful proximity of the word "ball". But she did. Eventually she started to call herself Margie, not Margie as in the song, but hard "g" Margie. She could see it and feel it.

Miracles!

My Good Intentions

I SOON REALIZED THAT THE TIME THAT I HAD TO SPEND WITH MARGIE WAS TAKING LOTS OF ATTENTION FROM MY OTHER TODDLER, PAUL, WHO WAS ONLY TWO YEARS OLDER. So for the first time in my life I considered nursery school. I thought it would be that 'something special' for him and would be a good idea. I enrolled him in the Ivy League Nursery School in Smithtown. It had a good reputation and had bus service. The first day he went happily, probably as a result of my intensive orientation. I wanted him to want to go. But I had waited a little long with this decision and so it was after the beginning of the regular term. The school didn't mind. No problem. So off he went on the bus that first day and I was jubilant.

But the next day he fought and screamed and didn't want to go. But I insisted. Oh what a mistake! But thereafter he went without too much complaint. It was only years later that he told me that that first day when all the other kids knew where they should go he didn't and he was left in the schoolyard for, well I don't know how long, but to him it was a terrible, long time, frightening and awful. And every time he comes to Smithtown to visit which is pretty often he makes a point of driv-

ing past the Ivy League School with his three girls
and by now they all chant together the terrible
tale. Of course, I know that he is teaching them
never to keep a terrifying event secret as he did,
but to make sure they understand they should tell
right away. But each time they pile into my front
hall telling me again how they now tell dad the
story of Ivy League, it always hurts anew. Regrets!

A Woman I Once Knew

VIVIAN CASH WAS CRIPPLED FROM BIRTH OR FROM A DOCTOR'S MISHAP OR POLIO. She walked with great difficulty. It wouldn't be right to describe her that way. Not only because to call someone a cripple is considered somehow not nice, but also because an individual's first and most outstanding characteristic should be the beginning of our personal description. So while she was crippled she was not a cripple to me. She was the mother of ten children, but that also should not be how I begin my description.

She was someone who radiated an inner happiness that was truly beyond description. Perhaps it was her physical disability that had caused her from childhood to rule out for her any possibility of a normal love life or family. Perhaps it was that love for that tall, straight and strong man, Joe Cash, a teacher, a part-time real estate salesman, a full time summer fisherman, helped to make her the luckiest woman on the whole earth. And she seemed to feel that way every day.

Whatever the reason, she was one happy person and fun to be with. She was short, a little round, with full rosy cheeks. Of course - she didn't, - no, she couldn't, drive. I met her first at a Rosary Altar Society meeting at Sts. Philip and James Church, shortly after we moved into Dogwood Drive.

Her husband had been the salesman at the builder's model house that we wandered through one day while we were waiting for a real estate agent to show us a house that would be ready that July when Larry was to start in his new medical practice. I'll never forget my unrestrained delight that day at the model, four bedrooms, two and one half bathrooms, on a half-acre of wooded property and all for the grand total of $22,990. It was like a dream come true, but we needed to get into the house by July first. Maryann was due in August and Larry was to start work July first, so any new house was out of the question. I had moved too many times to even consider a rental. But like a good salesman, Joe Cash, on hearing my unrestrained ravings about how this was the house we were looking for, handed me the papers and half kiddingly said, "Well then, sign here."

"Oh no, you don't understand, we must be in by July first."

"No problem," he said. "We have two houses up and ready for finishing and they could be ready for July."

He took us up the as yet unfinished street and into the house which only needed wall boards and cleaning up and otherwise it was finished, including an ugly pink bathroom and all. Of course, the end of the story is that we moved into that house on June 26, 1961, and have lived there happily ever since. And the pink bathroom has been replaced.

But I diverge. It's Vivian I want to tell you about. She was not yet in that category of friend, although our knowing her husband and maybe getting him a piece of whatever commission was involved bonded us a little. But it was several meetings of the altar rosary women later, when Vivian was absent, when the president announced that Vivian had breast cancer and she needed people to drive her to Huntington Hospital several days a week for radiation treatments.

It was then that our relationship changed. Quickly a group of us women decided on a schedule of drivers and for the next several months I got to know Vivian much better. Her cheerful demeanor never changed, in spite of the rumors that circulated that the cancer had already metastasized and while she had had a mastectomy, the radiation was really an exercise in futility. But we, in our turns, took Vivian to Huntington. Her youngest child was still a baby, two or two and a half. Money was very tight for them and as I remember health insurance even for teachers was rather sparse. But no complaints were ever heard from Vivian.

And then that once in a lifetime miracle happened. Vivian started to get better. It couldn't have happened to a better or a nicer person.

We kind of lost track of each other over the next four or five years, since they had moved to a house in Port Jefferson near the harbor where her Joe could tend his beloved boat, The Port Jeff Ace, a fishing boat for hire in the time when fish were still being caught in Long Island Sound. All summer he worked that boat, with his boys as they grew into tall copies of their father.

Then the news came back to Sts. Philip and James that Vivian had had a recurrence, a second mastectomy, and that she needed people to stay with her, to baby sit actually since she was then pretty much bedridden. Again the group reorganized this time for a half day a week each. So every Tuesday morning, my two preschoolers and I would drive up to Port Jeff and visit, do wash, grumble about all those kids and the way they left their things scattered about and pretty much try to ignore the then rather dire future.

Things didn't look good. I remember she was supposed to get out of bed every day, so we made the dining room table, it was a big one, our marker. Once around was good, twice was even better and three was, well actually I don't remember any more than three.

On her bedside table, at home or at the hospital, there was always a can of tomatoes. I finally asked, "Vivian, what's with the tomatoes?"

"Oh they're from Joe. Flowers are expensive, you know, and he always said, 'I was his tomato.'"

Her indomitable spirit never flagged. Her oldest child, her Margery, was getting married and Vivian knowing that I had taken sewing lessons from my friend with the wonderful maternity wardrobe, asked me to make her a wedding dress. She was determined to go down the aisle albeit in her wheelchair for her daughter's wedding.

I quickly agreed. We discussed the fabric, decided on a pale blue satin, in the then current 'A' line style, which really did nicely to cover her steroid swollen body, and a small band of sequins for the neckline. It was really quite beautiful.

All went well until she laughingly told me, "It should be modest, you know, since I will be buried in it".

I assured her that I would refuse to make her a dress for her burial. For her daughter's wedding, but not for her coffin! How selfish of me! She was ready and anxious to discuss her impending death and I couldn't. And being Vivian she did not push me.

The day of the final try on I will never forget. She told me where her falsies were so that the dress would fit right and as I helped her into her bra I realized that the hole in her chest where the second mastectomy had been performed had never healed and she was actually breathing through that hole.

She wore that beautiful dress for her daughter's wedding riding, not walking, down the aisle and six weeks later she wore it for her burial. But in between she planned a thank you party for all her helpers, a/k/a babysitters and our children. The party was to be on Joe's boat. The kids could fish and we were to be together. She would provide all the food and she even promised that they would get her onboard. But that was not to be. On the assigned day she was taken to the hospital. The cancer had attacked her spine and she had fallen. When we heard the news everyone wanted to call it quits, but Joe insisted. He had promised her he would do this party. And so we did.

Several days later when I went to the hospital to see her, the nurse told me I couldn't go in until they had finished bathing her. So I sat in the corridor for what seemed a long time. Then the nurse came and asked my name and when I told her she said that Dr. Werner was on the phone and wanted to speak to me. He was her doctor and she had died while I waited outside her room.

I don't ever remember a complaint. How could she not have been in pain? I don't know. To the end she was feisty. When the doctors' offices would call about bills she would tell them all, that they would get ten dollars a month until the bill was finished (which would probably take half a century) but not one red cent if they called her again.

In my religion we have saints and most of them are single nuns and priests who lived centuries ago. But I knew a real saint and will never forget her.

EASTER – MARCH 26, 1967. FROM L. TO R. STEVEN, LITTLE LARRY, MARYANN, MARGIE, MARY, PAUL AND KEVIN. BIG LARRY IN THE BACK-GROUND AND SNOW TO THE SIDE.

On Turning Forty

IN STARTING TO CLEAN OUT AN OLD FILE RECENTLY I CAME ACROSS THE FOLLOWING POEM I WROTE IN 1973:

On Turning Forty
It's Spring and my son goes to his first formal
tux and ruffled shirt
matching her dress
smiles, snapshots, strange feelings.
The telephone bill is seventy one dollars
I harangue and cajole and threaten
And Larry looks lovingly and whispers
"Don't you remember?"
"wait a minute, it's not time.."
The baby's in second grade
And I must be getting back to the world
and I am afraid
"wait a minute it's not time.."
So often now I look longingly at him
And see a tired reluctance
And remember, hurting, all those earlier times
The other way around.
Till now life's ebb and flow have carried me mostly
forward
No more carrying now

Time for me to ... do.
"Happy Fortieth Birthday, Mary"

"No, no, wait a minute, I'm not ready, it's not time."

A friend of a friend had just started a course, "Career Counseling for Mid Life Women" and I took it. I am not sure whether it was as a gesture of support for her or whether I was really ready to do something. When I had quit college after three years so Larry could go to medical school, I had promised myself that when I grew up I would go back and get my degree, but not until I knew what I wanted to do with the rest of my life. So here was my opportunity to find out.

The course was given by a psychologist and there were five women of various ages and backgrounds. We spent three hours each week doing a lot of what can only be called psychological games: what do you like to do, what do you do well, why do you like to do those things that you do well, etc. and each week when I would come home, Larry would say, "And so what did you do in school today" in mock parody of our own questions to the children over dinner each night.

After about four sessions when there appeared to be no hope of resolving my particular dilemma, she announced that we would do a dream sequence. Without regard to education, expense, experience, family obligations, without regard to anything we should tell what we would dream of doing, what we wanted to do, what we would like to be, even if it were in the realm of the impossible.

Without a moment's hesitation, I said, "Oh I would love to be a lawyer".

"Well," she said, "your problem is solved."

"Oh no", I quickly answered her, "I have seven children, and the oldest is a junior in High School and there is only nine and one half years between him and Margaret, the youngest, and there is no way we can possibly afford to send me back to school at this time. We don't even know how we are going to send them all to college."

She smiled with what I have begun to recognize as a purely psychologist's smile and said, "Oh, I think you should talk this over with Larry."

As women do in these situations we had gotten to know each other's husbands pretty well. And so, of course, when Larry dutifully asked what I had done at school that night I told him of this conversation.

"Do you want to be a lawyer?" Incredulous would not really describe his tone of voice.

"I would love to be a lawyer, but that's not possible".

"If you want to be a lawyer, you will be a lawyer. We will manage to put the kids through college somehow."

And we did and I became a lawyer and two of the children are lawyers, and three are engineers and one a social worker and one an at home mom who has her own radio show and astronomy club and is planning to build a planetarium in Athens, Ohio, and is a part-time tax preparer in season.

Forty was just the beginning!

My Bon Vivant

H E WAS QUIET. He was uncomfortably quiet. After the fall down the stairs at St. John's or rather the "catch" my good friend, Ruthie Dolan, and I would sit anxiously at a table in the cafeteria during the magical hour between three and four and hope to meet some of the guys. Me, I was really waiting for Larry to sit down and he often did but he was so quiet that conversation soon degenerated into us girls kind of babbling to fill the void. But I soon realized that while we were uncomfortable with his quiet, he was not.

He was funny, but in a low key kind of way. All the dances at college were formal and they required a corsage. Larry finally asked me to a dance. I was thrilled. "What kind of corsage would you like?" he said.

I quickly inventoried all the kinds of flowers. The usual gardenias I hated. They quickly turned brown around the edges and looked particularly funereal. The smell was heavy like a cheap perfume. But what to ask for? What would be the least expensive?

I quickly decided that violets would be perfect, different, pretty and how expensive could they be when I knew that they grew wild. But the dance was in January and as a Brooklyn girl I didn't realize that violets in January might be the most expensive flowers in the shop. Larry showed up for the dance with, of course, a gardenia. Oh well.

But then he produced another package. It was an African Violet in a small pot. Was I to wear it? Carry it to the dance? Or just put it on the table at home? When I looked at him quizzically he just said, "You asked for violets" and he smiled.

This was the start of a lifelong love on his part of African Violets, and a budding understanding on my part of his funny, wry sense of humor. He used to take violet cuttings from the most unlikely places, stick them in his pocket, bring them home and they would grow. And then he learned that he could take a cutting from almost anything and it would grow.

He loved to make things grow. He still does. We have plants in every room in the house. After he mastered the violets he started cutting all sorts of things. We have in our house the ugliest plant in the whole world. It is called a Night Blooming Cereus. It blooms once a year at midnight. Larry got it from someone, a patient I think, as a cutting. It is a kind of cactus that forms the flower bud on the side of the wide flat cactus like leaf, but before it does, during the long winter months and before that once in a year function, it puts out three foot shoots in a kind of cockeyed up and down spread, and grows in the most unlikely, dare I say ugly, shape. It is definitely not pretty.

But as "the night" approaches that it will bloom, from the side of one leaf starts a white limp bud that grows straight down. It starts to swell and then to lift itself in a curved form. It grows for several days swelling, becoming firmer and as it swells it becomes a graceful six or seven inch "S". And then "the night" arrives. We stay up and sit outside on our lawn chairs, with bug spray and flashlights. By now it has become a neighborhood party. As it starts to open it is upstanding, the fragrance is magnificent, the form like no other. The petals which have formed the swollen bud start to slowly peel back and become a seven inch wide gorgeous lily but in the midst of this forming lily is a field of stamens, hundreds of them, which are guarded at the entrance to the pistol with a beautiful delicate grid like web that is obviously designed to catch the moth not so as to kill it but to collect whatever it is that the moth is supposed to deposit on the stamens that wave gently in the breeze. They are so beautiful. Morning comes and it is limp, finished for another year. Anyone else would throw this ugly, once a year bloomer out, but not my husband.

He was hard working. He worked for forty four years as a family doctor in Smithtown. When people ask now "What king of a doctor were you?" His answer is always the same, "A good doctor." And he is right. He was a good doctor. In the early years he would deliver babies. He would set broken bones in the office. He had an x- ray machine and an electrocardiogram. He knew when it was appropriate to refer a patient to a specialist. But more important he knew his patients. He started as an employee of another family physician in Smithtown and soon became his partner.

Their work schedule was by today's standard very onerous, but he never complained. Hospital rounds every morning, home by twelve o'clock, lunch, back to the office for visiting hours until six o'clock, dinner, at seven back to the office for evening hours. And when he came home at ten or ten thirty we had a switch on the cellar stairs that he would click and all calls after that would ring directly in the house. His philosophy was that if someone were sick enough to call the doctor in the middle of the night, he should answer that call. And he did. But he had one protection against falling asleep during or right after the call. The phone was always on my side of the bed so he had to get up out of bed to answer it and by the time he came around the bed he would be awake and thinking clearly.

He made house calls. One night when he was out on a call the phone rang. The woman was frantic. Her husband was burning up. She didn't know what to do. This was in the time before everyone called 911 and got the volunteer ambulance to transport them to the local hospital.

"Is this Mrs. Werner?" she said frantically.

"Yes, but the doctor is out on a call. I will have him call you as soon as he gets back." This would not placate her. So foolishly I explained that when my children got temperatures my husband would recommend that I put them in a tepid bath and let them play and splash around until the water cooled and their temperature usually went down also. She was so grateful. I went back to sleep.

My husband returned home careful not to wake me. It was six o'clock the next morning and the phone was ringing again. "I am so sorry to call again, but my husband is shivering so badly. Can I please take him out of the tub?" That was when I told my husband about the earlier call. He graciously covered for me. I have never again to this day given medical advice, except to my children who accept it and then ask for their dad to confirm.

He has never arranged a vacation, but when I do he always enjoys himself. For my seventy fifth birthday I hinted broadly, very broadly, that I would like for him to arrange a vacation, maybe a river cruise in Central Europe. As the day approached and I knew that no such arrangements had been made, he asked me if I would like to go out to dinner for my birthday. We go out to dinner a lot. This was nothing special. I said," Yes!" and he asked, "Where would you like to go?" and I answered, "Prague", and so we had a quiet barbecue on our back deck.

Several years ago we did the death planning, executors, wills, power of attorney, health care proxy etc., etc. thing and I wrote a letter to all my children that I considered very clever. I wrote that their father and I were now ready to die and I gave them all the details of our legal arrangements. I sent a copy of this letter to my brother, Brother Ed. As soon as he received it he was on the phone laughing and congratulating me for such an intelligent and open letter. "What did the children say?"

"Nothing! I have heard nothing from any of them." He couldn't believe it. When I finally confronted one of them he said after seeing the opening paragraph, he put it away and said that when the time came he would read it but not any sooner. I felt cheated. I had worked on that letter, tried to get the right lighthearted tone while giving them all the necessary details.

Shortly after that, Larry and I had occasion to be in a very old cemetery upstate. There were lots of sayings on the grave stones. I asked him, "If you could, what would you put on your gravestone?"

Without a moment's hesitation he answered, "He was a BON VIVANT". I couldn't believe it! To me a bon vivant is what we used to call a gay blade, a ne'er do well, a party guy, a moocher.

"No," he said. "A bon vivant is a person who has lived good." He paused, "A good liver."

The First Daze of School

I WENT TO THE PUBLIC SCHOOL AT THE END OF OUR BLOCK FOR THE FIRST DAY OF KINDERGARTEN. The teacher was very stern and definitely no fun. After a couple of weeks the Catholic School, Our Lady of Angels, opened their kindergarten. It was in a separate house on the adjoining street and the teacher was Sister Mary Catherine. She was the kindest and sweetest woman I had thus far met in my life. I loved her. The best first day of school I ever would have.

Then there was the first day of real school. The nun's name was Sister Chrisentia and she was mean. She had sixty kids and on the first day she decided that Herbert Keating was "the bad boy" of the class and she promptly hung him in the coat room by the neck of his shirt and tie. Oh, not so that he would really choke just so that he and every child in that class would live in abject fear and terror of her and would never, ever forget her or her mean ways. I didn't even dream of telling my parents.

Then there was high school and suddenly the nuns were human and fun and anxious for us to learn and besides I had a friend from my street who was going to the same school and was six months ahead of me so she knew the ropes and was my kind guide. Ruthie Dolan was her name and she was in the orchestra, so of course I joined the orchestra putting my name in for the piano which by then I had mastered pretty well. But Sister De La Salle gently informed me that there was a plethora of piano players (I am sure she didn't actually use that word) but she would very much like for me to play the violin. When I protested that I knew nothing of the violin she informed me that if I could play the piano I could certainly play the violin and besides she would provide me with an instrument and give me a few lessons and that was the end of that.

For four years I played that infernal thing and all the time knew just how awful I sounded. But Sister was not to be deterred. She actually recommended me for the all-county orchestra which only increased my torment. It really was a great lesson in coping. Early on we learned that while we bowed furiously in practice, we gently pretended during performances to Sister's consternation. "Oh, Girls! I just don't understand it. You sound so much better, louder in practice. It must be when all those people fill the auditorium that it soaks up the sound."

"Oh yes Sister. That must be it," we chanted in unison.

Then there was college. St. John's Teachers'
College out off of the Myrtle Avenue El in Brooklyn, 4 to 10 every day and all day on Saturday and
in the same building as the Day School which was
all men. What a wonderful relief after four years of
all girls. My sister, Joan, had been there for three
years before me and so the first day and every day
was fun and besides I met my Larry. Basketball
games in Madison Square Garden, beer parties at
the local bar, Lutz's, and lots of formal dances at
the New York hotels. It was a little like being a
prisoner suddenly let loose.

We girls figured out a system whereby we could
have a different dress for each occasion keeping
track of which dress went to which dance with
which guy, being careful to guard against repeats.
Quite the fashionistas, we were.

Twenty years passed, babies, marching, peace,
war, Shoreham, migrants, meetings, demonstra-
tions and in the fall of 1973 my next first day of
school at Dowling College. After my epiphany
vocation event, I spent that summer getting my
twenty year old transcript, enrolling at Dowling which was close so that I could be home for
the kids after school, and enjoying the great satisfaction of being able to take courses I wanted.
So long as I took a year there, Dowling agreed
to give me a B.A. in Humanities. After I selected
courses that I really wanted, I had to take one

psychology course. Having been involved in lots of small groups and knowing that sometimes the spark would ignite and sometimes it just wouldn't, I saw a course described as the Dynamics of Small Groups in the Psych Department. Perfect!

So I was on my way to the future. But there was a little glitch, a happy glitch. For the first time in our married life I had planned for us to take a real vacation, just the two of us and Ireland was the destination and the first two weeks in September was the time. It was wonderful, but it meant that I had to miss one week of school.

Dowling College is on the old Vanderbilt Estate in Sayville, a happy conglomeration of buildings. Of course, I was early for that first day after missing the first week, but after I found the right building and then the right room, time was slipping away and besides the room was empty. Back I went to the Registrar's Office and then to the correct building and to the room which was upstairs. The building was a kind of two story cottage. Now I was really late. This was the Course on Small Groups. As I tried to creep into the room, I realized that this was no ordinary classroom. It was like a bedroom and arrayed around the perimeter were students in straight back chairs and on the floor sat more students. It was awfully quiet, when suddenly from a scruffy looking individual seated on the floor in the corner came a booming voice, "No late registrations!" I don't remember if he actually said "get out", but that was the clear import.

"Oh, I am already registered, just missed the first week."

"Then sit down."

One of the kids got up and offered me his chair. This was not an auspicious start. But worse yet this was followed by silence, deafening silence. Now, I was completely flustered. No one said a word for the next forty five minutes, not the rough voiced "teacher" in the corner, not any student, no one. Forty five minutes of silence! By the time the class started to break up, I flagged another "older" person and whispered, "Was it something I said?"

"Nope. We did this last week too. Crazy, huh?"

After several weeks of silence I figured this was the teacher's way to get us to start the group discussion going. I made several attempts to the dirty looks of the other students. After my second feeble and futile try to get the conversation going, one of the students approached me after class and said, "Don't you know, lady, this is the way it's supposed to be. What are you trying to do here? If you didn't want this then you should not have registered for this course." As though I were disturbing the peace! My only regret is that I lacked the intestinal fortitude to report this professor to the Dean.

And so went my fifth first day of school.

And then last but not least there was the first day of law school. I have no specific memory of that day. I have often said that law school was an exercise in medieval sado-masochism. We had actually competed to get in and then subjected ourselves to humiliating, abusive interrogation by our professors after spending every waking minute except the commuting time trying to read volumes of information about exotic subjects written in what to us was a foreign language. Oh and the commute: anywhere from one hour and ten minutes to three and a half hours on the Northern State Parkway. In desperation I finally tried reading the UCC out loud into my tape recorder and tried to listen to the tapes on the way to and from school. Now there was an accident waiting to happen.

And, of course, once home there was supper and homework and basketball practice and band concerts, etc., etc. I remember sitting way in the back of the Junior High Auditorium for the Holiday concert with my little flashlight trying to read law books during the performance. Law school was a nightmare, but those nuns many years earlier had taught me nothing if not endurance. As a mother of seven I remember feeling so discriminated against because the exams were held after the Christmas break so that all the single students had two weeks to study and I had Christmas to do. School days, school daze, good old golden rule days!

Am I happy I did it? In the words of a famous Alaskan, "You betcha!"

COLLEGE DAYS (1954) – PICTURED FROM L. TO R. RUTHIE DOLAN, MARY AND LARRY

Rackets Bureau

RACKETS BUREAU! The cache, the gravitas, the just plain "cops and robbers" of those words took my breath away. After a year and a half in the Suffolk County District Attorney's Office as the oldest newly graduated lawyer, after a year in the District Court Bureau experiencing the sharpest learning curve of my life, after four months assigned to the Grand Jury Bureau, I was to become the first woman ever assigned to the Rackets Bureau.

In the District Court Bureau I learned how to try cases, misdemeanor cases, but real trials of real defendants. As I remember I tried 37 cases in those fourteen months. Why? It was really in my power to avoid trials by offering easy plea bargains. But I didn't do that. I knew that trying cases was what I really loved to do and I wanted to learn how to do it well and the only way was by doing it.

The Grand Jury Bureau was where you handled arrest cases that were felonies and you had to present the evidence to the Grand Jury in order for them to vote indictments. The former Chief Judge of New York State, Sol Wachtler, has famously been quoted as saying that a District Attorney could indict a "ham sandwich." This was an obvious exaggeration, but not by too much. The presentation was completely one sided with the DA putting the evidence and witnesses in very abbreviated form in order simply to show that a crime had been committed and that this defendant had committed that crime in this county.

But now I was being assigned to a real bureau, a place where an entire squad of police and detectives were assigned to work directly with the DAs and various investigative tools: search warrants and wiretaps that the DA had to draw, were used. Here one was responsible to direct the investigation and to help determine when an arrest was warranted and even more important, timely, since many times if an investigation was terminated too soon the real "bad guys" would not be caught or if, on the other hand, it was delayed too long someone might be seriously hurt.

This really was important work. The office was located on the seventh floor of the H. Lee Dennison Building. The lawyers' offices were around the perimeter of the floor and the center was the "squad room", with desks for the detectives. Along the far wall were the secretaries' offices and the wiretap room where at any given time there were several taps going with the assigned detectives listening and trying to decode conversations. The rules were quite strict about what could be listened to. If the conversation was about the kids going to a birthday party it had to be cut off. After a short time the detective could again listen searching for pertinent conversation and follow the same procedure. Tedious work and frequently after several days it would become apparent that the kids' birthday party was actually a code word for drugs, guns or other contraband. One of the most interesting conversations that I overheard involved two mobsters discussing what they would wear and what presents they would bring when one of their friends was going to "be made". Becoming a "made guy" was a big step. It was the closest to the movies that I came.

For one of the years while there I worked in conjunction with the New York State Organized Crime Task Force. We had thirty five wiretaps going at one time. There was one tap in the car that the Suffolk Boss was driving into the City Boss weekly, loaded with bags of cash from the garbage bid fixing scheme in Suffolk County. We had one terrific informer who was 'inside' and who provided very good information. He was killed. And when he was killed the federal authorities got involved and while we turned many indictments the Feds using our evidence and after several years finally indicted the main man for murder. He may still be in prison.

I remember when my father heard that I was going to Rackets; he didn't like it at all. He said words to the effect that those guys were for real and they were dangerous. He was right.

One night while I was working late in the H. Lee Dennison Building just as I was getting ready to leave I received a phone call from a defense lawyer who I knew. He told me that "This phone call never happened. But my client just left my office and he said he was going to kill you." And then he repeated the first, "This phone call never happened" and hung up.

As the first woman in Rackets there was always the feeling that I had to be a little tougher than the guys. But that night I went into my boss's office right away to report this very upsetting call. He said that he had also gotten the same call and the same threat and that I was not to worry about it. It was just a lot of talk. As I got ready to leave the office, the Detective on the case told me that he would watch me go to my car. But what he meant was that he would watch from the windows on the seventh floor while I went down in the elevator alone and out to my car in the darkened parking lot. I always wondered what he would do if someone accosted me in the lot. Just how long would it take him to get downstairs? But that particular night I was really nervous. So as I got to my car I looked up and there was the Detective and he waved and yelled good night to me and I started home.

Very quickly I became aware of a car behind me. Was I being silly? No. It was pretty close. Did I turn and go to the Fourth Precinct which was across the highway? No. There is something about "home" that signals safety and security at a gut level even when it's not true. What was I going to do when I got to the house? How fast could I get my key which was attached to my car key and get to the front door? That car was still behind me. It turned onto Route 111 and then Dogwood Drive. It was pretty close. I was really afraid, really afraid. But I went as fast as I could. I was going home no matter what. I remember thinking, how was Larry going to fight off this thug. Uh, Oh! Was Larry even going to be home? Jumping out of my car in the driveway, the car that was following me pulled up slowly in front and the driver, my friend Detective Glenn Molyneaux waved and said, "Good night, Mary." I have never had such a strong urge to kill someone. My boss had assigned him to follow me home. Why he didn't tell me I will never know.

I was in Rackets for four years and had become deputy bureau chief; I remember the Sunday night that my boss called to tell me that he was assigning me to the Family Crime Bureau and that didn't sound so good at all since at that time in the District Attorney's Office, Family Crime was considered the Gulag of assignments, somewhere you went if you had screwed up. But David, my boss, said no I was to go as Bureau Chief. Again the first woman Bureau Chief in Suffolk and so I said "Great" and it was.

The Summer of 1980

THE YEAR IS 1980. It's summer and it's hot. I've been in Rackets just over a year. Suddenly a surprise, a very pleasant surprise. I've been selected to attend the New York State Organized Crime Seminar at Cornell University Law School in Ithaca, New York, for a week. Usually one or two lawyers from the office get to go, but for some reason that year there are eight places and so while still a rookie I am selected, me and seven guys were going to go away for a week. This would be only the second time in my life that I would be going away by myself. The first time was to Hong Kong with three officers' wives for four days and this was to be for a whole week to Cornell with seven young guys. And I was forty seven years old!

Two weeks earlier, my son, Kevin, had gotten married. They were just going to get married. No fuss. But I said if they were going to get married there should be a celebration. I volunteered to do a small reception at home. But our family and friends and the kids' friends and the bride's family and all of a sudden there were one hundred people. And the bride had two sisters and Kevin had two sisters and four brothers; the "small" wedding quickly morphed, four attendants, four grooms-men, dresses, flowers, etc. I hired two ladies to serve, but cooked turkey tetrazzini myself. It's funny how some things stick in your memory. I don't think I ever cooked turkey tetrazzini again.

The wedding was held at the Church of the Resurrection in Smithtown at twelve noon. I had borrowed tables and chairs and china since MY tetrazzini was not going to be served on paper plates. I had gotten three rolls of pink double knit from a cousin who worked at Staley Silk at a time when they were just going into double knits. It was fifty inches wide and so I just cut the table cloths to size, no hemming necessary. Pink geraniums wrapped in silver tin foil with pink candles turned my front yard into a very presentable reception area. We rented a tent for the backyard for the bar. (Those pink tablecloths are still being lent out. Double knit is truly indestructible.)

The ceremony was to be at twelve noon. Greek Catholic services are not noted for brevity, but I do remember that when we returned from the church the candles were melted over in all sorts of grotesque shapes.

Everything went well, food was served buffet in the house and the guests went out to the front yard tables. Wedding cake had just been served when a sudden and severe summer storm blew up. It was August. The wind was so strong that my boys all had to hang onto the edge of the tent awning for several minutes. They had a ball! The storm passed but most of the guests left and so there remained the real party people and a good time was had by all.

The next week was spent returning all the borrowed things, tables, chairs and china. And then it was time for Mary to go away, to go away with the boys.

The office provided two cars and the group quickly divided into the "A" car and the "B" car. I was assigned to the "B" car naturally and a blood oath was executed before anyone left Suffolk. No one under any circumstances was to speak about anything that was said or done that week at least the non-legal stuff. Some of the guys had been to the seminar in previous years and my presence seemed to frighten them a little. Ergo, the oath.

We were housed in the law school dorms. Breakfast was provided by the School of Hotel Management whose students were using us for practice and it was delicious. For dinner we were on our own and that is where the veterans were helpful. They knew which restaurants were good and which clubs stayed open late and they also had a reasonable knowledge of the back roads. Each night at dinner the boys introduced me as their mother and that it was my birthday. The presumption was that that would ensure free dessert.

It took one of them finally looking at the bill after three days for them to realize that they were paying for the extra cake and so that was the end of my birthdays.

I was a city girl. I had gone to St John's University Teachers' College located on Lewis and Willoughby Avenues in Brooklyn, a really nasty section near the Myrtle Avenue El. To say that I was very impressed by Cornell especially the Law School would be a terrible understatement. It was on the old part of campus, beautiful grey stone buildings, tall arched ceilings, windows that cried out for stained glass, Ivy League all the way. The Law School was located beside a gorge and the sound of the bubbling brook below was the breakfast accompaniment outside the dining room on a stone patio.

This seminar could only be described as a "gold standard" seminar. Each year it was devoted to a single topic of criminal law that was new and challenging in some regard. That summer it was going to address the new RICO statute and it was to be conducted by the author of that law, Professor George Robert Blakey.

RICO was a relatively new tool for prosecutors. Racketeer Influenced and Corrupt Organizations Act was the official title and the Suffolk County prosecutors were very interested in how that Act could be used in the unfolding investigation of the Southwest Sewer District.

While we eight partied every night, some later than others, not one of the whole group missed a single lecture, a testimony to the intelligence of Professor Blakey and the hard work of his law students who organized and indexed a fabulous resource book that was required reading every night and which served as a valuable text for many years to come.

That summer Larry, Kevin and Steven were already out of the house. John was struggling through a five and a half year program at the University of West Virginia. People told me later that it was the #1 party school in the country. And when John brought home for Christmas a bottle of white lightning to be mixed with Cool Aid as the drink of choice I began to realize the truth of the ranking. But he graduated and has been a happy employed engineer ever since although he still wears his cowboy boots every day. Maryann was at Siena College and Paul and Margie still in high school. But on December 8th, 1980, Dustin was born, my first grandchild and this past week as we all celebrated his thirtieth birthday with his mom and her sisters and his half-sister and her new baby, and his father, I looked back fondly on that memorable summer. I think my feeling was one of just plain WOW!

My Platinum Record

ONE DAY IN RACKETS, A COMPLAINT CAME IN FROM THE RECORDING ASSOCIATION OF AMERICA, NOT ONE OF OUR USUAL COMPLAINANTS. The case was assigned to me and I set up the usual initial interview. The gentleman who arrived was dressed in rather conservative business attire, but was accompanied by a youngish, more casual, colleague. It turned out that they were bringing a criminal complaint that there was illegal, unauthorized copying of certain records, significant and successful recordings, which of course, resulted in rather substantial monetary losses to the companies and artists involved.

The Recording Association was a business association which had been formed by the big recording companies to fight this kind of unauthorized and counterfeit recordings and the sale of such. Any time there was a big concert, there was an announcement that any recording of the performance or any part thereof was not authorized, etc. However, there were several fairly talented individuals who not only overlooked these admonitions, but proceeded to record the whole concert and sell it as a separate and special recording with no remuneration to the performers who, of course, were not in the poverty mode, but were in the business of making records and money and were very careful concerning their branding if one could call it that.

The case was already fairly well prepared by the Association's lawyers. They had the original records and the fakes and they knew pretty much the individuals who had been stealing and selling them and so all that was involved for me to do was to put all this before a Grand Jury and seek an indictment. I don't think the intent was to seek jail or even fines but simply to scare these individuals into compliance with the rights that legally were to go to the composers, performers, and recording companies.

The really interesting part of the case was that I had to put into the Grand Jury sometimes the performers themselves; the records that were the legitimate records and then play the fakes and then produce the Expert or the performer who was to testify to the obvious (to them) differences between to two and that constituted the case.

But of all the assistants who might have had a clue to who the recording artists were and which recording was real and which was fake, the very last person in the whole world was me. While other much younger assistants were wildly enthusiastic about having some of the performers actually come into the office and then to the Grand Jury, I was the least informed and the least interested, which was probably the reason I was assigned. The boss didn't have to worry about me trying to take any of the evidence, not of course that any other assistant would do such a thing.

And so I spent hours in front of the Grand Jury which was composed as it usually was of older citizens who didn't want to, or were not clever enough to, get out of serving for a month instead of the usual one or two days. If I didn't know any of the names of the actual artists most of them likewise were not interested until that is, they had told some of their grandkids who they saw in the Grand Jury that day. It seemed that as the presentation went on their interest started to improve.

But we, or I should say, I slogged through many days listening to what the experts testified were clearly not the real thing when in truth I couldn't tell and could just about stand listening to the music. I wish now that I could at least remember the names of the stars involved, but I can't. But I do remember, after the indictment was voted and the matter was resolved to everyone's satisfaction, a large group of the bigwigs from the association came into my office and presented me with a platinum record, beautifully framed in honor of all my efforts on their behalf.

I still have the record although the frame has been lost. The real value of it was (it's not real platinum) that I hung it in my office when I went to Riverhead as a Judge.

Before any trial would start there would usually be a conference in my chambers, to settle any legal issues and/or to try to actually settle the case. It was always fascinating to see the two or three lawyers trying to convince me of some esoteric point of law involved in their accident or malpractice case. They would usually sit on opposite sides as they faced my desk and the record hung on the wall to my right so it was visible usually to only one of them and not to the others and to see that one's eyes stray to the record and then do a double take looking at me again and then to see them lose completely their train of thought and to see the opposing lawyer or lawyers on the opposite side of the room who didn't have a clue, looking startled and quizzical listening to the argument that had started perfectly logically and turned into a mish-mash until the opponent simply couldn't hold it in any longer and asked, "Judge, when did you get your platinum record?"

It was a wonderful conversation starter and many of those otherwise unsettle-able cases ended up settling. Of course, most of the lawyers knew the songs and the artists and were all too happy to talk about the value of those unauthorized recordings of the whole concerts which they had treasured as teenagers.

Family Crime

IT WAS A SUNDAY AFTERNOON WHEN DAVID CALLED WITH THE NEWS OF MY NEW ASSIGNMENT. An indication of the low regard that the Family Crime Bureau enjoyed was that I had no idea where their offices were even located. But I was going to be a Bureau Chief and I had the distinct feeling that the only direction the Bureau could go was up. David was the Chief Assistant and when I asked if he had told the existing Bureau Chief about the change, he indicated that that fellow was on vacation and when he returned he would be informed. Not the best way to get transferred and his new job didn't sound like a promotion.

So next morning I got into my car and went looking. I knew that at that time the Family Court Building was located in a string of old Quonset huts at the back of the property on the north east corner of Old Willets Path and the Smithtown Bypass (Rt. 347). In the front of this block was the Suffolk County Legislature Building. And right on the corner was a big red brick building that everyone referred as the Old Fourth Precinct. It was unoccupied at the time.

Sure enough, at the very western end of the Quonset buildings, way in the back, was a building labeled Children's Shelter. It was pretty dilapidated and at that time I was not even sure what the Children's Shelter was used for, but I did know that it had been closed by the State as unacceptable housing for a Children's Shelter. But there was a small unofficial looking sign that said Family Crime Bureau.

So in I went. Right as I opened the door there were a series of desks in the hallway on the left for the secretaries. The building was oblong in shape and on the right side of the hall were the old cells with the bars removed where the children had been housed. These were the Assistants' offices. In the corner of each there was a little baby toilet. In some rooms there was an attempt, mostly by the female assistants, to camouflage them, tablecloths, flowers or plants on top, but the guys seemed to glory in the unseemliness of having a visible toilet in their offices.

As I greeted the first secretary, I realized that it was Kathy Nappi, an old friend from Rackets. She had been the Chief Investigator's Secretary, a most prestigious position which she held until she dared to get pregnant and although she was not demoted when she returned from maternity leave, she was assigned to Family Crime. Enough said.

As she recognized me and realized the reason for my presence there even without my actually saying anything, she leaped from her chair and started to dance down the hall announcing that Mary was going to be the new Chief. It sounds a little far-fetched, but she literally danced down the hall announcing my arrival and she was joined by a chorus of greetings that spoke of hope and expectation on the part of everyone. I knew all the Assistants and the detectives and the investigators. It was an astonishing start.

I realized that my first job would be to get this group out of this depressing place which evoked a bad message in a loud voice not only to the workers but to the victims and their moms, a message that Family Crime prosecutions were not important.

But they were. They were the most difficult and important prosecutions that I had ever been involved in. They were cases of mostly single women, moms with their children who had been abused by their boyfriends, their daddies, uncles; babies, young children who had great difficulty expressing what had happened to them. Many had to deal with the fact that their mother didn't really believe that her lover or husband could do this to her child.

More than any other kind of case we needed hard evidence, but at that time Child Protective

Service was mandated by law to respond within 24 hours of the report of abuse and they were not police people and didn't have any real idea of the importance of collecting evidence: panties, pajamas, sheets or anything that could be tested to tie the perpetrator to the crime. We had a pediatrician who was available to examine the children, but the fact of vaginal or rectal trauma was not enough. We needed the testimony of the child which was very difficult to obtain since most of these little ones felt that somehow they were to blame. If there was hard evidence it was much easier for us to obtain convictions.

So my first decision was to form a committee composed of the Child Protective Services (CPS) Supervisors, the Police Captain who was in charge of the Unit that did the investigations and in some rare cases arrests, and the assistant DA's (ADA's). At first it was tense. A blame game. If you had done or not done, etc., etc., we could have gotten him, but all these players, these individuals had the same objective, to stop the abuse, to assure the safety of the child, to get the guy, and to make sure that it didn't happen again to this victim or anyone else. It took a few meetings and finally the tension in the room dissolved, "Oh, I didn't realize that you had to do that or needed that." Or words to that effect. CPS has a very long and complex law mandating them to do certain things within certain time limits and the police likewise have guidelines. Sometimes these can be contradictory in the short run or at the least impeding successful prosecutions. But eventually they developed a congenial understanding and a relationship that recognized the difficulties of each other's obligations.

But child abuse was not the only part of our mandate in the Bureau. We were responsible for prosecuting cases of domestic violence. The challenge of many of these cases was the fact that there was a relationship between the victim and the perpetrator and that relationship had always started with love, then violence followed. April La Salata was the classic case, the extreme case. He killed her. We had three domestic violence homicides within a three week period the year (1987) that she was killed. In those other cases of abuse, frequently by the time we would be before the Judge asking for high bail, showing evidence of serious bodily harm, the victim would appear and beg the judge to let the defendant go. He had called her from the jail and was so sorry and she needed him to support her and the children, etc. The Assistants got very discouraged very fast.

That first Christmas at a Bureau meeting I announced we all needed a party, bad! Immediately of course there was agreement and I volunteered my house. The detectives, said they would do the cooking and after setting a date within the week, asked for my house key and off they went on the appointed day shortly after lunch and by the time the staff: ADA's , secretaries, Investigators, all of us got to my house there was a sumptuous Italian feast and presents for everyone, fun presents. I don't know how they did it but it was a wonderful morale booster

The gifts were the funny kind that only detectives can come up with. The one I remember most, since I have a picture of it, was my secretary, Kathy, sitting on the hearth in my family room, blowing up what the detectives called baby condoms but, of course, were little finger cots that are used medically if a finger gets cut. Laughter is really the best medicine especially for a group that feels that no one appreciates what they are doing and how difficult it is.

Quickly I found new quarters for the Bureau in the Old Fourth Precinct Building. The upstairs were old cells with the bars still intact but there was a spacious basement that was at ground level, bright, sunny , lots of windows and rooms that lent themselves to office space. We even had an extra room which we painted bright yellow as I remember and installed hidden video equipment so that when the little ones came in they could play and then gently tell their story to our children's advocate, a delightful young woman and

the ADA assigned to the case. And we could vid-
eotape their telling.

One of the advantages of this location was that
it was not in a courthouse and so when the kids
came in they came by the downstairs backdoor
and the whole feel of the place was non-confron-
tational not threatening. In order to hook up the
video equipment my son Larry came in one Sunday and after disconnecting the whole New York
State System, reconnected it and it all worked.
When I mentioned our Sunday escapade to someone in the then newly spreading computer section, he nearly had a heart attack since he was
convinced that no one like my son could possibly
do what he had done successfully. I think he was
reassured when I promised not to tell anyone.

I remember that Sunday and while Lil Larry
was doing his magic, Big Larry who is several
inches shorter than Lil Larry helped me to wash
the windows and paint the walls in my office. I discovered that such improvements are contagious.
The other offices suddenly started to appear on
Monday mornings in new and different colors. It
was beautiful!

One of the hardest parts of the job was to introduce young, mostly female attorneys to the horrors
of the crimes we dealt with. But we also had some
guys who had as much trouble as the women. I
remember one day my secretary, Kathy, saying to a

new female assistant who was a real blusher, that she should go into her office and close the door and just say "penis, penis, penis" until she could say it out loud without even blinking. And then "vagina". This became a kind of office lore but in the repeating it was a way of recognizing for each new attorney that everyone had difficulty saying such words in court without blanching and blushing.

Although dealing with cases of children being sexually abused and women being beaten and sometimes killed was very hard, I look back on my role as Chief of that Bureau and remember the terrible fear, fear that we might not succeed, or that we might prosecute the wrong person. In some cases the "would be" defendant was a respectable member of his community, a teacher, a pediatrician, a dentist, a businessman. It was my job to decide whether to bring charges or not. Was there sufficient evidence? Could we get a conviction? I remember one case that involved a policeman and it went to trial and he was acquitted. As the child left the courtroom with her mother, she whispered to the ADA, "Please help me." She knew that with the acquittal there was no reason for her step-father not to have access to her. While the mom had started divorce proceedings the fact of that acquittal became a strong argument for the father to gain custody with his accusations of the mom instigating false charges against him, using the child in such a way, trying to alienate the child, etc.

And so there came a day or I should say there came many nights when I decided I could no longer do it. It was time for a change, but what could I do? Almost fifteen years in the DA's Office. I could try cases, I could prosecute cases, but I didn't think that I could become an effective defense lawyer as many ADA's did. So I decided to become a judge. And that is another memoir.

Why

❧

IT WAS THE THIRD OF JANUARY, 1987. I was at home around nine thirty, dinner finished, dishes done and all quiet. The phone rang - a sound that sets off those little bells of apprehension when it is after the hour of social calls. I quickly picked it up and heard a familiar voice, "Hi Mary. This is Frankie Morro". Frankie was a detective I knew from my work in the Rackets Bureau of the Suffolk County District Attorney's Office where I had been assigned for eight years. I now headed the Family Crime Bureau. He was a really nice guy, a kind of gentle person one doesn't expect as a detective. The tone of his voice told me something was really bad.

"You guys working with a La Salata case?"

"Oh no! Did he kill her?"

"Yeah. I am so sorry".

"Where?"

"Right outside her house as she was coming home from work, shot her three times in the head". I started to cry. I don't think I have ever cried so hard. Tears of grief and loss, but more tears of fury, of frustration, of the senselessness of her death.

April La Salata was 34 years old, in one way a classic domestic violence victim, in that she had married young, suffered the gradual escalating signs of her husband, Anthony's, domination. Insults, slaps, and pushes led to serious injuries that required emergency room visits, but always with him at her side so that when asked what happened he could say how she fell down the stairs. And each incident, each assault, was then followed by the "So sorry." "It won't ever happen again" "I love you" "Please forgive me".

But she was different. Somehow she found the strength to say "Stop!" She filed for divorce, obtained an Order of Protection, got a job and went on with her life with her two children. But the day her husband, Anthony, was served with the divorce papers he changed her life forever. She was upstairs in her bedroom after work chatting with her young son about the day's activities. Suddenly her husband jumped out of her closet, attacked her with a knife and slashed her repeatedly. Her son ran downstairs to call for help, but Anthony had cut the telephone wires (that's called premeditation). He had forgotten the basement phone and the son called from there and saved his mom's life.

April spent the next four months in the hospital recovering. Anthony was arrested and held on bail. As soon as she was well enough she would come to our office and talk to the ADA assigned to the case, Fran Radman. She was ready and willing to testify. More than that, she was anxious to tell her story and to get him behind bars for at least a long time. It was what we call in criminal prosecution an "open and shut" case. The trial would not take very long.

That did not happen. A judge reduced the bail. Anthony got out and then started to stalk her. Each time the case was on the trial calendar we would ask for a trial and each time the judge would grant an adjournment at the defendant's request. Finally, April asked if she could speak to the judge and we assured her she could. To no avail.

The next time the case was scheduled, she came into the office and showed us a photograph which she had had taken. It was a full frontal picture which showed her, all ninety pounds of her, in small bikini panties with each hand over her almost nonexistent breasts and the scar which ran from the base of her throat to the top of her pubic area. There were three or four other scars where he had slashed at her. It was the closest thing I had ever seen to an autopsy photo. "Show this to the judge. Maybe then he will understand. Please." And we did but he didn't seem to care. He claimed to be busy trying custody cases. On the day she was killed that judge had not tried a single case, in or out of custody, in the previous six months.

Meanwhile Anthony was stalking April, driving by her house when she was outside, leaving little signs for her to know he had gotten into her house, moving the lipstick, changing the placement of her personal things, demonstrating his control. We charged him with violation of the Order of Protection. The judge threw it out. We outfitted her with a personal alarm device. It was in her purse when he killed her.

The detectives who went to her house to install the alarm begged her to hide until the trial. She had a job; her two little ones were in school. She didn't want to give him that final control over her. She was the strongest woman, the most courageous individual I will ever know. And that night through my tears and frustration, my anger at a system run by the old boys, "manned" by the old boys, I decided to become a judge, to try to change the way women like April La Salata were treated.

In April of 2007, I was asked to sit on a panel at the Touro Law School on the topic of women in the judiciary. Since the topic was about women, most of the audience was female law students and female lawyers. Other panelists spoke of how they had come up in the system and what they had done to become judges and how many women there are now on the various benches. I told them about April La Salata and begged them not to forget.

Becoming a Judge

I PICK UP MY STORY WITH MY "DECIDING" TO BECOME A JUDGE. Of course that was the easy part. Although psychologically I think it was the hardest because in a very important way it was a surrender, a surrender to the horrors of the job of Chief of the Family Crime Bureau of the District Attorney's Office, to the difficulties of deciding the fate of individuals: babies, children, women, fathers, abusers, victims. It was a kind of "I give up." "I can't do this anymore." And giving up was foreign to me, but survival was more important.

So I started to scan the Law Journal for the announcements of openings for appointment to the Court of Claims and to get in touch with the schedule of elections to the other courts. I knew that I didn't want to become a Criminal Court Judge or a Family Court Judge either, that would be the same all over again although at that point in my professional career I was eminently qualified for those exact jobs.

The courts in New York State are a veritable jumble: Court of Claims is an appointed position and handles claims against the State, but after the War on Drugs gained momentum in the seventies it also became a court where the incredible increase of drug cases were to be handled by newly created Court of Claims Judges. The remaining judicial positions are elected: District Court, the lowest court, elected by Township; the Family Court, elected by County; and the Supreme Court elected by Judicial District, in my case that included all of Nassau and Suffolk Counties. And then there was the odd case of a judge retiring or dying in the middle of his or her term. (It should be noted that I use "his or her" in this case without meaning. They were all men. All his-es.)

I set my sights on Supreme.

The first step was to get the application that was uniform for any appointment to the bench. It was very long and very complete: employment history; cases tried and the names and addresses of the opposing attorneys and the outcomes; the Judges before whom you had appeared; membership in the local and state bar associations and committee positions, etc., etc.

I consulted with my boss, the District Attorney, James Catterson to let him know what I was doing and he turned out to be my best advisor. He was a Republican as was the entire bench in Suffolk County with the exception of a couple of Democrats who had been cross endorsed in the civilized days of Joseph Margiotta. No longer was that accepted. So I faced the remote possibility of an appointment or the impossible task of election.

I was a Democrat and a woman: two really huge hurdles to my becoming an elected judge. On the election road, my next step was to contact the Democratic Boss of Suffolk County, Dominick Baranello, since the only way one can get on the ballot for a Supreme Court position is to be nominated by the party convention which takes place in September for the election in November and the only way one gets nominated is for the party boss to approve that nomination.

I remember my first visit to the Democratic Headquarters which was located down Route 112 in a shabby two story house on the east side of the road close to Sunrise Highway. It was foreign territory to me. As a newly hired Assistant District Attorney back in 1977, the then DA, Henry O'Brien, asked us all to forgo all political activity since it presented an obstacle to our being perceived as impartial. It was no problem for me since I had never liked the "political scene" and so for the next fifteen years, with succeeding DA's, Patrick Henry, and Jim Catterson, I had continued my un-involvement. But now I needed to suddenly become really involved politically in order to get a nomination.

So after waiting a respectable time downstairs at headquarters and watching the rather frenetic

activity that I guess is part of any really political place, although I daresay the Republicans
are probably much better organized, I was summoned to go upstairs to speak to Mr. Baranello.
At the time I had that "kissing the ring" feeling,
but I was pleasantly surprised at the reception.
He was delighted to have me run. There were six
slots for Supreme Court that November and the
Democrats needed six lawyers to fill those spots,
lawyers who could pass the Bar Association's
Screening Committee. He seemed sure that that
would be no problem for me. I agreed although
my lack of civil experience might pose a problem.
His only condition was that I would not take the
Right to Life endorsement since the Democrats
were opposed to that party's position on abortion.

The next step was to get screened by the Suffolk County Bar Association Judicial Screening
Committee and that was another seventy page
application, but since I had done the one for
appointment it was not so onerous. At that time
there were three possible findings that that committee could make for a candidate: "Qualified" or
"Highly Qualified" or "Not Qualified". I had been
on that very committee and had been a founding
member of the Suffolk County Women's Bar Association; I had been on the Board of the Suffolk
Academy of Law and had held positions with various Bar committees. The Screening Committee

found me "Qualified". It seems that the "woman "part was the deciding factor between Qualified and Highly Qualified.

I was on my way. The Democrats didn't expect me to get elected. No one expected me to get elected. The Chair of my Committee to Elect Mary Werner didn't expect me to get elected. But Mary Werner expected to get elected. Greenhorn was a word that the Irish used to describe the newly arrived cousins from Ireland who didn't really know anything about America. I was a genuine Greenhorn to the political system and quickly began to realize that the Democrats weren't interested in wasting their political capital on a hopeless candidate. They did, however, provide me with professionally printed 'palm cards'. They had a couple of delightful young women out in Center Moriches do the layout and they did the printing in the basement of headquarters. But they would only give me five hundred at one time so I made many trips to Headquarters during the weeks that remained before election.

My Committee was composed mostly of non-lawyer women friends, people who took the job of campaigning very seriously. I had a friend from college, Maureen Keyes, who was recently retired from teaching, who said that she would ring every doorbell in Babylon Village and tell everyone why they should vote for me and who I was and what I had done and why the bench in Suffolk needed a woman and that I was that woman. My sister lived in New Hyde Park and she did the same. I had a friend whose sister was a Sister and she wrote to every convent and told them why they should get out the vote and who they should vote for. So many friends and unbeknownst to me all those women who had been working all those years for women victims and who had never had a sympathetic ear in the DA's Office until I got there, all those women were out there from one end of Suffolk to the other end of Nassau County working their magic, telling anyone who would listen that they needed to vote and to vote for me and only me. It's called bullet voting and gives the recipient six votes instead of one in the final count.

I spoke to any group of voters that were interested in judicial candidates. Not many really care. And then election night came. We were in Democratic headquarters watching the results. It was torture. It was close, but we lost, not by much, but we lost. But I was determined to try again and when I did I would know the ropes a whole lot better.

Becoming Continued

"**P**ICK YOURSELF UP, DUST YOURSELF OFF AND START ALL OVER AGAIN." So goes the song and so we went. My Committee to Elect was just as enthusiastic as before but once they found out that there were to be twelve slots for Supreme Court that following fall in the Tenth Judicial District, they were particularly hopeful of success since I had come in seventh out of the six slots that November. Anyone with political brains would know that our thinking was really addled, but it carried us through that spring and summer renewed and rejuvenated.

We went to any meeting that would give us a few minutes; I gave my spiel over and over: "Hi, my name is Mary Werner and I am running for Supreme Court and would like you to vote for me." One Saturday we went to the Smithhaven Mall and my good friend, Nina Pozgar, contributed at least a hundred helium balloons on the premise that the folks with children would stop and at least take a balloon and maybe give me a chance to introduce myself.

We, as lawyers, knew that we couldn't do the pamphletting inside the mall but we felt there was a legal argument to do it outside on the sidewalk, a kind of public place. And we were hoping that on a busy Saturday the Security would be too busy inside and would therefore not have time to bother us. Of course, we were mistaken and no argument legal or otherwise would convince the police that we could stay. So in the midst of trying to unscramble the balloon strings and give them away as quickly as possible to avoid stuffing them back inside the cars and while Nina argued heroically with the mall security person, I gave as many palm cards away as I could, temporarily trying to disassociate myself from her to give me a little lead time. The end was a couple of middle aged women laughing hysterically and attempting to get the remaining balloons into our cars before we got a couple of tickets for Illegally Congregating or some such thing.

Not all our campaign stops were as much fun however, but all were more than a little discouraging. People did not really want to hear about Supreme Court Candidates. They just were not interested. But there was one special night. By then I was working in Riverhead and one of the Democratic judges, Al Lama, called me and told me that there was going to be a big "Meet the Candidates" meeting that evening at the Riverhead Gun and Hunt Club, not a usual Democratic kind of audience, but he assured me that it would be worth my while. A big crowd was expected.

So after driving up and down Route 24 looking for a sign of this Club, I finally stopped at the Crossroads Restaurant and asked the bartender for directions. He called the chef out and the chef knew the place, he was a member, and he gave me good directions. So I ordered a cup of real coffee, and a pack of Marlboros, sat for a few minutes, smoked a cigarette, collected myself and off I went. I was only an "occasional" smoker, but as the campaign went on the occasions multiplied.

I found the Riverhead Gun and Hunt Club that night. It was a large building back in the woods. It didn't have a proper parking lot - just places among the trees to park. It had a big meeting room that was set up with rows of folding chairs. About three hundred people were there. I was thrilled. Most meetings had no more than fifty.

As soon as I saw Al Lama, he started to apologize. It seemed that the organizers of the meeting didn't want to waste time with the candidates for Supreme Court having a few minutes each, so they had decided that they would announce our names and we could stand and that was to be that.

I was all alone and could see the Republican candidates in the front of the room standing there with their handlers, people who were there to drive them and to help hand out their material. So I quickly decided that this was not going to be a waste of my time. I went back out to my car, got as big a bundle of literature as I could carry, and went back into the meeting room. It was packed. The meeting had not started yet so I went from person to person, climbing over the people, stumbling over the folding chairs, and speaking to each and every one of them. Many were Polish farmers, and their wives. As soon as they saw my palm card which had a picture of me and my family, the women especially started to read it and to ask questions. "Do you have seven children?" "Is that you in the picture, you are much prettier than that." "What party are you in?" "How long have you been an Assistant District Attorney?" "I am going to vote for you." "I am going to tell my daughter to vote for you." They wanted to engage me in conversation and that evening I really felt for the first time that I had a chance, a chance of winning, if I could meet and talk to enough people. Of course when the women heard that there were no women on the court that was a kind of clincher. They were outraged to hear that.

In the middle of the campaign, I was summoned to appear before a committee to review me for the purpose of appointment to an unexpired term of Supreme Court. I went. The meeting was held in a very small meeting room of a very large, prestigious law firm in Manhattan. These committees are composed of a mix of lay people and lawyers appointed by different individuals as well as by the Governor. The elderly gentleman who was acting as Chair of the group started the proceedings off by asking me why I would want to do this. Why would he ask such a thing, I wondered. This committee was supposed to investigate my legal abilities and qualifications. He was the lay representative on the committee. There is a process that goes on inside one's head at times like that. It had happened to me on several occasions in a court room when a Judge asked a question that had nothing to do with the action, a kind of left field question and so figuring this interview was not going anywhere, I answered, "Why, sir, did I forget my makeup this morning?" Was he implying that I was too old for the job? I don't know, but it certainly set the line of questions askew.

They wanted to know about an investigation that was going on in the office that had nothing to do with me or my work. I figured that would be the end of me as a possible candidate for appointment. But the killer was the last question by the same gentleman who had started the proceeding. He said, "So I guess you will be marching in the St Paddy's Day Parade." I asked why he thought that and he answered, "Well, I see that you have seven children, so you must be Catholic and so you must be marching." I could not begin to figure how many Federal and State Statutes that his question violated, but I sweetly informed him that I wouldn't be marching.

I left the interview at least relieved that I would not have to decide whether or not I would accept an appointment if offered since if I didn't get elected in the fall I would be out of a job.

But life continues to surprise and amaze me and not too long after that disastrous interview, the Governor of New York State, Mario Cuomo, called me on the phone and offered me the position of Supreme Court Justice for the unexpired term that would run from that early June to the end of the year. I accepted. I can't really remember just what I said, but I do remember that I accepted.

So now I was campaigning as a Supreme Court Judge and boy did that make a difference, even though I was a Democrat, and a woman, and the only woman on the court. No women on the County Court. No women on any Court except one on Family Court.

It was a crazy, busy summer. The Democrats started to treat me as though I might actually do it, I might actually get elected.

Election night is a kind of blur. We were at Suffolk County Democratic Headquarters. We watched the machine showing the returns. It was very close. I was in twelfth position and then in thirteenth then in twelve. Back and forth and finally Suffolk County was closing their headquarters. They were throwing us out because Nassau had closed without finishing their returns so it was pointless to wait there until morning. I was thirteenth, but the Nassau returns were not in and they had closed.

The next morning Newsday had me as winning with 56,000 votes, clearly a completely useless story since the vote totals when we had left headquarters the night before were in the 200,000 range. The worst part was that people started calling me with congratulations. And I didn't know whether I had won or not. After a few frantic phone calls, I decided to call the Board of Elections. They certainly should know. So I dialed the number and a lovely lady answered. I told her that I wanted to know whether I had won or not. She laughingly asked me my name and what position I had run for. Soon she reported back that yes, indeed, I had won the spot for the New York State Supreme Court, twelfth out of twelve. I couldn't believe it. After hanging up, I suddenly realized that I had not even asked her name. ELA-TION! JUBILILATION! GRATITUDE! One is at a loss for words even now these many years later.

And so the next day we went on vacation to Ixtapa, Mexico. I think I called my secretary at least once a day to confirm that in fact I had won the election. I remember the phone service was terrible there. I had to use the phone at the front desk. It was located in the lobby of the resort. There were many large, loud parrots in cages in the lobby as decoration, I guess. But it was really strange; me yelling into the phone and asking the same question over and over and the parrots squawking at the same time. I fully expected that by the time we checked out the birds would be able to say, "Did I win?" "Did I win?" "Did I really win?"

JUDGE MARY M. WERNER - 1994

Music, Mind and Memories

Iᴛ's 2012. On a Friday night, not so long ago, Larry and I went to the annual fundraising concert and dinner of the Long Island Symphonic Choral Association, LISCA, at the Old Field Club in Stony Brook. The music was magnificent; a string trio played selections from Rollo and Beethoven. As I sat soaking up the beauty of the sound, my hands in my lap, palms upturned, I was suddenly stunned to realize that the music for me is only good for the moment. There is no memory of the actual experience, of the sound, no reenactment as it were. But sitting there my mind was filled with other days and evenings that were spent in that same spot.

The club is located on the creek in Stony Brook and as I looked out the windows to the back deck and water and the rise of land across the way before the gloom and grey of the evening closed off the view, I was back to an evening in 1991. The Suffolk County Women's Bar Association was holding its annual inauguration dinner. I was the outgoing President and had invited the Honorable Joseph Bellacosa, Associate Judge of the New York State Court of Appeals, truly a 'feather in one's hat' kind of speaker for that fledging organization.

He, a good friend of Larry's brother and my freshman New York Civil Procedure teacher at St. John's Law School, had accepted my invitation as a personal favor.

But even more special was the fact that earlier that day I had traveled to Albany and sat in the gallery of the New York State Senate with my husband and good friend, Elaine Ingram, as Senator James Lack put my name before that august body for confirmation to an unexpired term of the New York State Supreme Court. To the Senators in session, an ordinary vote, a murmured aye, no nays, and I was a JUDGE, but to me there was a feeling that can't really be described, but can certainly be remembered.

So that evening when Judge Bellacosa arrived at the Club, he quickly congratulated me and said that he would swear me in as part of the evening's proceedings. There were murmurings by people in charge about how that would somehow detract from the incoming president's evening. That was really unreasonable.

I was a founding mother of the organization, and the outgoing President. Our purpose as an association was to advance women in the law. I was becoming the only woman then on the Supreme Court bench. But I was so elated by the day's experiences I couldn't be upset by petty negative thoughts and Judge Bellacosa graciously offered to do it after the evenings' proceedings out on the back deck. It was a private swearing in ceremony. Jim Catterson was the District Attorney at that time and my boss and my guest at the dinner. He had been very supportive of my judge efforts over the previous several months even calling the Chairman of the Senate Judiciary Committee to introduce me. He was upset by the rebuff to me and the Judge, but I was on cloud nine and didn't want to entertain any negative thoughts.

Breathe deeply and realize the music. Oh the loveliness of it!

The music sweeps over me and is gone. But that evening, that swearing in evening, is as clear and real today as it was then. We went outside after the installation and speeches and there on the back deck in an intimate circle of friends and family, Judge Bellacosa administered the oath.

It was dark. The stars were shining. The joy of the moment, the realization of the life changing possibilities of the event, even the specter of the summer to come that would have to be spent campaigning ferociously for the position, could not dampen the experience.

And so began a new chapter.

MEMORIES, JUNE 26, 1991 –FROM L. TO R. DONNA WERNER,
DONALD WERNER, JUDGE JOSEPH BELLACOSA, MARY WERNER,
PAUL WERNER, LARRY WERNER, AND KEVIN WERNER

Hear Ye! Hear Ye! Hear Ye!

THERE ARE TIMES IN LIFE WHEN YOU ARE SUDDENLY CONFRONTED WITH A SITUATION; YOU ARE IN CHARGE, YOU ARE SUPPOSED TO KNOW WHAT TO DO AND YOU DON'T KNOW A THING ABOUT IT AT ALL – NOTHING. The clerk who had just explained that this was her first day also, asked if I wanted her to "bang me in".

Not knowing what she meant, I said, "Oh, yes." And then banging loudly on the door of the courtroom she announced in a very loud voice, "Hear ye, hear ye, hear ye, the Honorable Mary Werner" etc., etc. I don't really remember the whole announcement, but it surely meant that I was someone important and someone who was supposed to know what I was doing. And I didn't.

The usual practice in Supreme Court is that each judge can appoint his or her secretary and law secretary. This latter title is confusing since this person is a lawyer who is supposed to do any legal research that the judge may need and to do the paperwork of the part which is very onerous, lots of motions, actually hundreds, and to draft decisions for the judge's signature. We had been cautioned in New Judges' School to make sure that the person we appointed to that position was smarter than we were and the judge who said that was really serious. We had chuckled at the time, but as things went on I realized just how good that advice was.

I had received a call from the Administrative Judge, Arthur Cromarty, several days earlier while I was still searching for someone for that position, when he told me that due to budget constraints, I could not hire a Law Secretary, but that if I had any questions I could call on one of the lawyers from the Law Department. I did not know much about how things worked, but I was smart enough to tell him in no uncertain terms that I had to have a Law Secretary of my own. He quickly acquiesced.

But finding someone who wanted a six month job was difficult. Everyone knew or thought they knew that I was not going to be elected. Democrat! Woman! Not in this county! But I did find someone; a woman who it turned out was in the throes of a divorce and while pretty smart, was not too available mentally.

So after being scared out of my wits by the loud banging and furious announcement, I walked into my courtroom. It was located upstairs in the county center. There were two courtrooms and the most junior of the judges were ensconced there. At that time the Supreme Court was spread out all over the county, with four courtrooms in

Central Islip handling matrimonial cases, some in the County Court Building and the rest in the old Supreme Court Building on Griffing Avenue.

The courtroom was pretty small, but as I walked out I realized it was full. The only time a courtroom is that full is in arraignments or in a criminal case that's really hot. What was going on? There were local lawyers who I recognized, but as the others put in their appearances I realized that some of the names were famous individuals from Washington, D.C. representing the Board of a local bank that was a party in the case. And that the courtroom was full of young assistants, mostly male, all carrying large briefcases ready to provide legal help to their partners in the well. How I wished that some of them could come over to my side and help me to grasp the dimensions of the action and share their legal research.

In a nutshell the case involved an attorney who was the bank president, who had been asked by certain lawyers representing the bank's board of directors to answer questions in the course of a due diligence investigation. He went with a fellow lawyer, to the meeting and in the course of that meeting disclosed certain very incriminating things at which time the lawyers representing the board stopped the meeting and advised the bank president to obtain his own council.

The court action really involved whether or not those statements were privileged as attorney/ client statements. In the course of the hearing I sealed the courtroom and directed the bank president to answer the questions. Not really knowing the civil rules about this issue, I applied rules from criminal court proceedings and after a full summer on and off the case, we were affirmed in our decisions by the Appellate Division a couple of times

And so started the illustrious career of Justice Mary M. Werner. It was only later that I realized the assignment of a very complicated, politically hot and locally important case, and a brand new rookie clerk were all part of the "old boys" treatment of a new and female judge.

Two years later, I was appointed to the position of Administrative Judge (AJ) of Suffolk County. I was in charge of the "whole shebang", a prestigious and fabulous opportunity. It allowed me to introduce what was then a new and almost untried concept called Drug Courts, the aim of which was to rehabilitate drug offenders rather than incarcerate them. My position as AJ also allowed me to find room in the courthouse and funds to construct and furnish a children's room - a warm and sheltering place.

But lunchtime came and Judge Alan Oshrin who had the courtroom next door popped into my chambers and insisted that I join the "boys" for lunch. He was a delightful, smart and eventually good friend who saved me on more than one occasion.

Beginning The Beyond

I T WAS A FRIDAY NIGHT. I was still working in River-head, April 8, 2006, and it was young Larry's fiftieth birthday. We had been invited to a surprise birthday party for him out in Frenchtown, New Jersey where his then fiancé lived.

I usually liked to drive, but that night I was particularly tired. It had been a busy day in court and so I asked Larry if he would mind driving. He said of course not and he drove all the way out on that busy Friday night, through the city and out Route 78 in New Jersey to the party which was almost by the Delaware River.

After the party was over and we had finally settled into our hotel nearby, in the bathroom while we were getting ready for bed I noticed it, a nasty elongated bruise running from Larry's left shoulder to his right hip. "What happened? What did you do to yourself?"

In classic Larry fashion he said, "Oh, I fell in the garden today and didn't want to break my wrist so I put my arm across my chest." He must have fallen flat on his face.

"You fell! Why didn't you tell me you fell? I could have driven! We could have skipped the party! Was it a sugar episode? (He was diabetic.) What was it? What else did you hurt? Turn around. Let me see your back!"

When he met me earlier that night he had a band aid across the bridge of his nose and said he scratched it in the garden. I should have known!

The morning after we got back home I called his doctor who saw him right away, and got him to the cardiologist who scheduled him for an angiogram at Long Island Jewish Hospital on Monday, June 19th. The hospital was highly recommended and considered one of the best places for heart problems. Of course, Larry was awake during the procedure and interested in the TV images of his arteries. When he saw them he realized they were in very bad shape and he agreed to a by-pass operation which was scheduled for that Friday. His condition mandated that he stay in the hospital that week until the heart doctor, was available to do the operation.

It was a pleasant week. We met a woman we knew from our parish, a former patient of Larry's who had had a by-pass the week before and was in the Step Down Unit and recovering nicely. That unit was for post op patients, six beds in one room and lots of staff and monitors. We felt confident that Larry would get the best care possible. It seems strange now, but I really believed that Larry would survive the operation which had become pretty common by then. I had no fear of his dying. Perhaps I should have, but I didn't. Lots of our friends had had it and were fine. We actually didn't know of any fatalities.

But young Larry was concerned. One night that week as he drove me home to Smithtown, he said that he had called his siblings; he had decided that his brothers and sisters should have a chance to see their father before the surgery in case he didn't make it. I was shocked since the kids were spread out around the country, from Ohio, to North Carolina and the trip for many of them to Smithtown was difficult. He scared me since Little Larry was our half doctor, having served for many years as a paramedic and AEMT on the Smithtown Volunteer Fire Department Ambulance. He was always full of medical questions after his various calls and his father was always full of answers. So Little Larry knew what all those numbers on all those machines really meant.

On June 22, 2006, Larry had a quadruple bypass and spent the following day in the Cardiac Intensive Care Unit. It was one on one care and he had tubes from every orifice plus many others. And then good news, he was to be transferred to the Step Down Unit, surely a sign that he was doing well. We all took a break and then went up to that Unit. He wasn't there. They told us that there was no room there and we finally found him in a private room right opposite the nurse's station.

But it turned out that the proximity to the nurses' station meant nothing. As the hours went by and no one was checking him, in spite of my repeated requests, not even a simple finger stick to check his diabetes, I became frantic. As he awoke enough to hear my complaints, I saw and heard my husband yell for the first time in my life. I don't know where he got the strength to do it. "Get that nurse in here NOW!"

I think she actually heard him and she came and he yelled again in a louder voice, "Get the Head Nurse in here now!" As she tried to use that calming kind of nurse voice he yelled again, "Get the Head Nurse now or I am going to pull every tube out." Quickly the Head Nurse came and then the heart doctor and his coterie of residents arrived and closed the door and then all the tubes were removed and Larry completely exhausted finally started to sleep.

As I lay on the floor in his room that night and tried to get some rest myself, I realized that "good hospitals" are only as good as the nursing care. The next morning as I tried to talk him out of walking out then, I found on his night table a small card with information on Private Duty Nurses. "Who put that there?" "The heart doctor".

Was I supposed to have known that a private room meant that I was responsible for his nursing care? Why didn't someone tell me? Of course, then I retained private duty nurses. Larry told me the next morning that every time he awoke during the night the nurse was asleep and he didn't want to disturb her.

There was one more procedure that required that he be wheeled downstairs and on the way he met a lung doctor who he knew. A short conversation ended with that doctor saying, "Larry, get out of here as fast as you can before they kill you."

We went home with meds prescribed by the nurse practitioner in the discharge unit and on the tenth of July he was so weak that he needed hospitalization, an endoscopy to detect the location of bleeding and then a transfusion. Wrong meds? Who knows? I don't remember how many units he got, but I know it was more than one. He came home and started the long slow process of getting better.

He had retired three years earlier and seemed to have lost his interest in anything. Now I understood in view of the condition of his blood supply why he was so apathetic. He loved the garden, but when I suggested he might want to join the Round Table Program at Stony Brook University, he refused. We had a good friend, Joe Parrella, who was involved there and had tried to talk Larry into it.

But one Sunday in August while Larry was still in the tired stage of recuperation and sitting in the big chair sound asleep I called Joe and asked whether it was too late for us to enroll in the program for that fall. Joe was surprised, "I thought Larry wasn't interested."

"Oh no," I said. "He's very interested. Please send me the bulletin" and while I planned to retire myself I enrolled both of us in the Program, then called the Round Table, and subsequently renamed the Osher Life Long Learning Institute, OLLI, for short.

Looking at the bulletin and trying to find something he might be interested in I picked a course about Entropy taught by a Stony Brook physicist, Al Tobin, and a Memoir Writing course for me taught by two wonderful ladies, Sheila Beiber and Dorothy Schiff-Shannon. That was the start, that September of something new and wonderful.

He grew to love it and I grew to love it and that was the beginning of the BEYOND.

80TH BIRTHDAY PARTY, MARCH 17TH, 2012 – FROM L. TO R. BIG LARRY, LITTLE LARRY, KEVIN, MARY, EDWARD, STEVEN, JOHN, MARYANN, PAUL, AND MARGARET

The Piano

I CARED FOR THE FAMILY PIANO FOR 46 YEARS AND PLAYED IT FOR THE 20 YEARS PRIOR. It was entrusted to me. It was mine but not really.

It was about eleven o'clock in the evening, and I, having put off as long as possible, the job of sorting the piano music, was doing it at that late hour. Suddenly I was sobbing uncontrollably, and I might say, uncharacteristically. Why? I had given my piano, no THE PIANO, to my son who had made arrangements to have it moved to his house the next morning. So why the crying?

I think I had begun to realize, to really realize, that none of our prized possessions are ours for good. We are just caretakers. The piano was the piano that I, as a child, had played for all the Sundays that I can remember at Nana's.

After my Grandmother and Mom and Aunt would have prepared and served the dinner we would all go to the living room where the piano resided in an alcove and I would play to the best of my increasing ability the "Irish Songs" and they would sing. As time went on I could play Chopin and Tchaikovsky and Schumann and my piece de resistance, the Kamenoi-Ostrow. But my folks

were not really interested in those pieces and so
I saved my accomplishments for my own pleasure
and that of my teacher

When I went to St. Saviour's High School and
they asked who wanted to play in the orchestra,
I, of course, signed up. But there was a plethora of piano players so the music teacher whose
name was Sister De La Salle informed me that if
I could play the piano I could, of course, play the
violin. She needed violinists and so after three
lessons, I played the violin. Believe it or not I
eventually became first violinist in that orchestra and the worst part was that I knew how awful
I was on that violin and how sad that orchestra
sounded.

This special piano sat in the alcove at Nana's
house for all the years of my growing up, never
tuned but played at least weekly. I got married,
went to the Philippines, had four children and
finally prepared to move to a brand new house
in Smithtown and was expecting my fifth child. It
was the spring of 1961.

I had little time to think of this piano that had
been purchased by my Uncle Robbie, my Mom's
brother, for his first wife, Mae MacBain, as a wedding present in 1928. Mae was my Mother's dearest friend and she died a year after her marriage
of "heart trouble" and my Uncle Robbie and his
piano moved back into my grandmother's house.

He eventually married again, but his second wife came with a fully furnished brownstone house including a grandmother and an uncle. He did not want the piano and as long as my Aunt Kay and Uncle Bill lived at Senator Street they had no objection to the piano staying right where it had been those many years.

Around 1953, my Mom and Dad moved for the first time in my memory to 928 80th street between Seventh and Eighth Avenues. Both Joan and I were married and had several children and by 1961, Larry and I finally landed in Smithtown ready to move into a brand new four bedroom Colonial.

Before we could move to suburbia, however, the ground floor in Mom's house in Brooklyn became vacant and so it was the natural thing for Aunt Kay and Uncle Bill, Mom's sister and brother, to move in. By then both my grandmother and grandfather had died. But Aunt Kay, usually fairly low key and quiet, promptly announced that she was going to tell Uncle Robbie that, "I will not pay to move that piano!"

Half kidding and rather flippantly, not having seen it in a very long time and having all those fond memories and all that, I said," Well, you tell Uncle Robbie I'll be happy to take the piano". I had no idea what was involved in moving pianos and in storing them since this was all happening while we were waiting for the new house to be completed.

As fate would have it when she called Uncle Robbie, expecting him to come and get it or sell it, he said, "Well, wouldn't that be nice. Tell Mary she can have it."

My sister, Joan, came to the rescue, as she often did. She offered to have it moved and stored and delivered to our new house. She said it would be her house warming present. What a wonderful gift! I was thrilled and delighted and could hardly wait.

June 26, 1961, we closed on the new house and even before that date we had moved in. The street was not finished and the lawn not in, etc. but we were safely in our rather bare but spacious house and the next baby, number five, was coming in August, so I was anxious to be settled.

The day came and the piano arrived. Oh, what a terrible disappointment! This piano had been neglected for 30 years; the finish was a mess and the contrast with my new living room was dramatic.

My husband was a general practitioner who came home for lunch every day. He never said much about it, but he could read my pain every time I saw what looked like a monstrosity in the living room. And every day at lunch time he would take out a bottle of lemon oil and his drill with a pad on it and he worked on that piano in twenty minute intervals for months, until it shone and looked as grand as it sounded. And many years later for a birthday present when the sounding board cracked, he had the whole thing refinished inside and out. It was grand in all respects.

The piano gave me so much pleasure over the years. It inspired almost all of my children to need music in their lives growing up and some of them still continue most especially my Maryann. She was born in August, my first girl.

So when we were writing our wills, out of all my things, nothing was worthy of separate legacy except the piano which I bequeathed that Maryann should get when we both died. It was several years later in an informal conversation when she said to me, "Mom, what were you thinking? I live in Ohio and I will just sell the piano. I couldn't afford to move it and besides I have no room for a baby grand."

I was projecting my feelings for the piano onto her. She's definitely not the sentimental type. I couldn't believe my ears, but she was right. It was silly of me to say she should get it just because she plays beautifully and accompanies not only her own children at concerts, but many of their friends.

And so rather quickly I decided to give the piano to my second son, Kevin. He lives in Stony Brook and had always half kiddingly complained of the piano legacy going to Athens, Ohio. At Christmastime that year, I verified that Maryann was serious and said to Kevin, "Well then, the piano will be yours."

I received a wonderful response, "Do you mean it? That's great! Thank you!" and so I was happy and after trying to play the usual pieces I realized that I could no longer do that, so I told him to take it now while he could enjoy it and I could enjoy giving it.

This morning at nine thirty the piano movers were here and took the piano to Kevin's house. Boy, does my living room look bare!

So here I sit trying to understand my feelings. What is this hurt in the heart over this hunk of hardwood? I have given away jewelry from my Mom and Aunt Kay and some of my own without a second thought. Why tears over the piano? As I carefully went through the music and separated the "Irish Songs" that I played all those years ago and the Beethoven and the Chopin and the pieces that I got from my Aunt and Uncle from the First World War and those pieces from the Second World War, my weeping intensified.

So guess what I think? The piano personified in some mysterious way the wonderful, persistent love of my Larry. He spent all those hours to make it beautiful, to make me happy with this, this wooden thing that made beautiful music.

But there's that other thing, the unspoken rebellion against the stiffening fingers, the loss of the ability to make the music. Could it be that I don't want to grow old? Silly question! Who does? I am getting old. The piano speaks to me of the flight of time. I will go to Kevin's house and hear him play and that will be wonderful. Life goes galloping on and we know that, but sometimes it hits very hard, kind of like in **BOLD**.

My Mother's Story

ON SEPTEMBER 25TH, 2009, MY MOTHER WOULD HAVE BEEN MARRIED EIGHTY YEARS. And so I begin her story.

This is not a memoir. It is impossible to write about my mother in that shortened form. This is my mother's story.

I have been writing my memoirs for three years now and have yet to write of my mother at least not directly. When I read my piece about Peach Taffeta Dresses last summer in the Memoirs Class, at the end of the critique someone quietly said, "How mean she was!"

As I drove home that day, that comment haunted me. Had I portrayed my mom in such awful terms? I had to write her story, the whole story, because she was in the words of the old hymn, "my rock and my salvation". But my mother was never mean. She was strict and straight and strong and firm and sometimes cranky, but never mean. She raised us to be strong and neat and nice and as smart as we could be, but she was never mean. She never put her arms around me and said, "I love you." But she was never mean.

In second grade the nun told us that we should
go home that Valentine's Day and tell our mothers that we loved them. I struggled all day because
those were not words we ever used, until finally
when she was tucking me in for the night I said,
no whispered really, the words. "I love you."

"What did you say?" I repeated them, quietly.

"Oh that's nice. Now go to sleep."

I never said them again. She loved us, me and
my sister and my brother. She never told us that,
but as I got older I realized it in a new and clearer
light. She loved us very much and I am glad she
and I lived long enough to realize that and to
experience it in so many ways. Writing about it is
very hard. We never did talk about it.

I recently heard a commentary on NPR by
a man who had written a book on his WASP
upbringing. He was commenting on how they
never talked about sex or love or really any emo-
tion. They never talked about "those things". I,
born of Irish immigrant grandparents, was a long
way from WASP, but we also never talked about
"those things". Perhaps it was the time and cul-
ture of that generation, rather than any particular
heritage or person.

She was a paradox, my mother. While I say she
was strong she took many years to overcome her
own devil of alcoholism but she did it and she did
it alone. That devil was as a cloud, a dark cloud

over my childhood. I was in high school before I realized what it was that was changing her. From day to day I wouldn't know whether she would be my mother or that other person I hated. I never told anyone about her drinking until I was pretty sure of my Larry and then I told him and of course he said that it didn't matter. But it did matter. Every day it mattered.

The night before my wedding as I ironed my borrowed wedding dress, I prayed and prayed that she would be sober at least for the reception. How selfish I was. I didn't really care about her or her needs; it was all about how it would look if she were drunk. I so wanted things to be right and proper. Was I my mother's child?

But as adulthood overtook me, I began to realize the kind of love she had for me. Strong, firm, straight, generous. No hugs, no soft words. She wanted us to have a life that was easier than hers. And if there was a way that she could help us to have that, she would. It was never a question of money since she and Dad had very little, but rather it was the very personal giving of herself, when I needed her for babysitting; watching the seven kids for two weeks when we wanted to finally take a real vacation; filling in when I went back to school and always without any talk. She just seemed to know when I needed her.

One of my children's favorite memories of my mom is of her appearing on a Friday night with my father on a surprise visit and in her pocketbook she had a smoked tenderloin or two, and her own peeler since she knew that I would always have potatoes. That way there would be a dinner that she would cook to make things easier for me. And in her shopping bag she had her house dress at the ready.

When strangers meet me and find out that after seven children, I went to Law School, became an Assistant District Attorney and then a Judge, they ask how did you ever do it. My reply is always that my youngest daughter, Margaret, my deaf daughter, taught me that I could do anything. In teaching her to speak, I learned that I could do the impossible. But that is only half of the story.

While Margie taught me that I could do anything, my mother was there to help me to actually do it. My mother was there when I needed her, helping me with all the ordinary things, encouraging me without ever saying "Go for it." or "I love you." She made it possible.

So who was she? She was born on November 2, 1901, All Souls Day, the oldest of four children of Bridget and John Powers both born in Ireland. She had one sister, Catherine and two brothers, Robert and William. My grandmother, Bridget, took William/Bill to Ireland for a summer visit when he was eight. He was her baby. The family matriarch in Ireland, Aunt Statia, who was childless, persuaded Bridget to leave Bill for one year and come back the next summer to take him home. And so she did. But by the next summer Aunt Statia would not let him go home. So Bill grew up in Ireland until the outbreak of the World War when he was convinced that he should come back or lose his citizenship.

What kind of mother gives up a son, her baby? My grandfather had a pretty good job working for the NYC Parks Department. Poverty was not the excuse. As kids we just knew that Uncle Bill had grown up in Ireland, a fun and interesting fact, but as a grown up the whole idea was starkly wrong.

My mother's mother, my grandmother, Bridget Daly Powers, was frail, barely five foot and no more than one hundred pounds, obviously easily bullied. But I have documents that show that she was the Secretary to the Tipperary Football Team Society, so as a young immigrant mother she must have had some gumption. And, of course I have already told the story of her and the stove in the Highlands.

My Mother was always a little on the plump side. A clean starched house dress, to be distinguished from a house coat, was her usual garb and when she would come to Smithtown to stay for a few days to help, she would have a freshly starched house dress in her shopping bag. She was never to be bullied.

There was a settlement house in Mom's neighborhood when she was growing up, called Friendly House. It was run by two single ladies, the Miss Sphinxes. They ran programs for the Irish immigrant community in downtown Brooklyn. Mom lived on Warren Street.

During the summer the Miss Sphinxes ran a camp in a place that I think was called Congers in the Catskills that consisted of tents for sleeping and a house for cooking. There was a lake nearby and lots of space for the city kids to play and to learn to swim. It was a safe place away from the threat of city diseases and especially polio. According to my mother and Aunt Kay they had many good times and lots of fun there. The mothers and children stayed there all week and the men came up on the weekends.

These tents were the source of my mom's awful fear of lightning. She must have felt so unprotected during the terrible summer storms that blew through the Catskill Mountains. During the winter, Friendly House had cooking and sewing classes, musicales and shows. Uncle Robbie and Aunt Kay took violin lessons and performed in the shows. There were Irish football teams. When the young girls were ready for their first job, one

of the Miss Sphinxes found an appropriate placement for them and accompanied them to their
first interview. They found my mother her first job
as a secretary.

Mom had graduated from Bay Ridge High
School and she kept that secretarial position for
ten years. An indication of the regard with which
her fellow workers held her, when she married
they bought her a complete set of Noritake china,
service for twelve, as well as a set of stemware:
wines, waters and cordials all rimmed in beautiful gold. These were, of course, the "good dishes"
that only came out of the china closet on special
occasions. Actually, whenever we ate in the dining
room that was an occasion that was special.

My Aunt Kay, Mom's sister, was likewise introduced to her first job at Kendall Mills where she
worked for fifty years. She was a single lady and a
marvelous Aunt.

I don't know when my mother met my father. I
think it was at the Friendly House Summer Camp.
He was very good looking, an orphan, who graduated from St. Peter's Grammar School in New
York City. He didn't have much of a job, but he
loved her very much and was willing to do pretty
much anything to win her. Her one condition
was that he "go on the police", about the only job
for young men who didn't go to high school. He
fought it because growing up poor and orphaned

on the streets of New York and Brooklyn, to him the police were the enemy, hated by all, especially the kids. Cops were violent and mean and corrupt. Of course he finally gave in and was sworn in as a New York City Police Officer. He married my mom on September 25, 1929. The "Crash" occurred that October.

After they married and we were old enough to hear the occasional argument, I remember my mother begging him to do the collections of the "bag money" for the sergeant as the sergeant had ordered. Dad refused and was actually docked several days' pay in punishment for it. She argued that the sergeant would get someone else to do it anyway and we could not afford the loss of pay. He didn't care. The shopkeepers were supposed to be protected by the cops and not be paying for that protection. He would not participate in that dirty work.

Although my mother never talked about it very much, I think the Depression days were very hard. There were unpaid leaves, which meant you worked but didn't get paid. I think she felt bad complaining since she knew so many who didn't have a job and in the police at least when the leave was over you were sure of a job and a paycheck.

In the years before she married when mom worked, she saved enough money to furnish the first apartment and to invest a little with her cousin, also called Robbie Powers who worked on Wall Street. Her small nest egg was lost in the crash.

My father didn't ask much, but he insisted that once they were married, my mother should not go to work, that he could take care of her. As an orphan who never knew a father who could take care of his family he was determined that he would and he did. As it turned out, my sister was born eleven months later so it wasn't an issue. But now I wonder how my mother felt about not working. Later, when we were all in school it was not even considered that she would go back to work. My father wanted desperately to be able to support his family and he did. But in later years when my mother turned to alcohol I wonder whether his insistence on her staying home didn't add to her unhappiness.

After my mom's death, I found letters between her and May MacBain, her very special girlfriend. The letters were filled with silly fun, so light-hearted. You can almost hear the giggles between them. This was a different person from the person I knew as a child. May married Robbie, Mom's brother, and died a year later in February 1933, from rheumatic heart. I was born that June and was named Mary. My mom never told me the connection, but as I try to reconstruct her life it is very apparent that I was named for her good friend and sister-in-law.

She raised us to behave, to study hard, to be neat and to be nice. I don't think we ever sat on the living room couch. We played on the floor. (Note: None of my children ever sat on our living room couch either; am I my mother's daughter?) Joan and I shared a bedroom and a bed. The apartment only had two bedrooms. My brother, Edward slept in a crib in mom's bedroom until they moved to another apartment at 928 80th Street, also in Bay Ridge.

My mom was a person who believed in spring and fall cleaning. The heavy drapes were taken down, the windows washed, and the curtains washed, starched and dried on the curtain stretcher, an instrument of torture. I remember the pricked fingers and then the blood stains on the edge of the curtain. But it wasn't only the curtains that were stretched, the lace runners as well. The stretcher would have to be adjusted to the right size, the nuts and screws undone and redone and all the while handling the wooden bars with the pins just waiting for your fingers. But that was not all; there were heavy winter rugs to be taken up, hung outside on the back line, and beaten, wrapped and stored in the basement and replaced with the light straw summer rugs. And then, of course, the process was repeated six months later.

For my mother, housewifery was a full time job; that is until my baby brother arrived in 1940 when Mom was 39 and 3/4s years old.

I was seven when my brother, Edward, was born. My life changed. I should say our lives changed. He was what my mother called a "change of life" baby. I don't know, since she never discussed it, what form of birth control she used, but she had such faith in it that a pregnancy at thirty nine was in her mind impossible. In later life she told me that our doctor, Dr. Lane, thought in the beginning she might have a tumor instead of a pregnancy.

Edward was a big baby, cranky as anything, but the love of my father's life. If he cried and he did a lot, my father would insist that it must be a diaper pin sticking the poor baby. He would undress him; change him and when the crying continued, my father would decide that it must be the rough seams on Edward's little under-shirts. So Edward always had his undershirts on inside out.

When Edward was almost two, he came down with what I believe was thrush, with a very high temperature that ultimately left him deaf in one ear. But Mom didn't know it then. As he got older, he was the tallest kid in his class and it became apparent he was not as smart as his two sisters (at least that was the conclusion when he had trouble in school). No one even considered the idea that he could not hear and could not improvise with learned lip reading from the back of the class-room.

After Edward entered the Brothers at sixteen, the Brother in charge told my mother that he had suspected a hearing problem and when they had Ed tested they found a complete loss in one ear. My mother was furious. It was as though someone had proved that she was a bad mother. It was funny, since Edward was relieved to find out why school had been so hard for him, but she was so insulted to think that she had not considered what was by then so obvious.

Edward is now a Ph.D. and incredibly successful in his chosen religious life.

When Edward was approaching four and still taking a bottle, another sign of maternal failure, Mom decided that she would tell him no Santa Claus unless he gave up the bottle. What a mistake! Christmas Eve came and Edward couldn't go to sleep. He cried and cried. Of course, he wanted his bottle but he was old enough to know that he wanted Santa more. My mother finally said ok and tried to give him the bottle but he wouldn't take it. She had done a very successful job of convincing him.

My mom became an alcoholic. I'm not exactly sure when. There were times when I would come home from high school when she would be her real self. But other times she would be a person that I did not like. By the time Edward, who is seven years my junior, was in high school she was so bad that she would be staggering. I hated the person she was when she was drinking.

My mom had first cousins, Alice, Margaret and John. Their father was a full blown alcoholic who went on benders for two and three weeks at a time and would return all loving and nice and sober for about two months and penniless. We didn't have a telephone so Allie would occasionally come for an unannounced visit. When my mother would see her coming up the driveway with the kids she would moan, "Oh my God, it's Allie!" As a child I found this reaction confounding since Allie and Mom would then sit at the kitchen table, have a beer and start talking. They obviously would be having fun, laughing and having a good time until dark. What Mom told me many years later was that she dreaded Allie's visits, because when she would be ready to leave she would ask Mom for money and, of course, Mom would give her whatever she could spare and then would be short for the next two weeks until Dad got paid.

My relationship with my mother started to change when I married Larry. It is only in hindsight that I begin to see why. She knew he was going to medical school and that someday he would be a doctor and that we would not have to worry about money the way she did. But she also really liked him.

She didn't come often to Manhattan to our first apartment, but once we moved to Flatbush she figured how, using two buses, she could come even when my father was working. I can't describe the relief I experienced on her visits. I have struggled to find the right word, but relief says it all. I was suffering from thyroid disease that was as yet undiagnosed and tired was my fulltime condition. When I would tell my doctor, he would answer that, of course, with all those babies I should be tired. She would pitch in, whatever needed doing she would do and do it willingly, almost gratefully.

Little Larry was born thirteen months after our wedding; Kevin thirteen months later; Steven eleven months after Kevin. Kevin was a difficult baby, perhaps because he came home from New York Hospital with a staph infection that required several weeks of antibiotic medication; after that he developed a full body rash that was resistant to all the then known treatments, we changed his diet, his milk, he lay under special lights all to no avail. I remember going for a doctor visit, I think Kevin was about nine months, and the pediatrician gave me a tube of ointment and said it was very new and dangerous that I should be very careful with it. It was a miracle. In two days the rash was not only gone but his skin looked like a lovely baby's should. The ointment was Cortisone, now sold over the counter. I think the year was 1957.

While the treatment finally worked, I think he had forgotten how to sleep in the process. He would cry. Those three words just cannot describe the torment of a cranky baby, an uncomfortable baby. He was a screamer. We had to separate Kevin from Larry and then Steven so that they would not all cry at the same time and wake each other up. This took some doing in a one bedroom apartment.

Little Larry would sleep in the large bedroom in his crib with a stool fan purring year round since we found it helped him to get to sleep. Kevin would sleep all bundled up in the front hall which had no heat and Steven would sleep in the bassinet in the kitchen beside the washing machine. He was a sleeper. It probably was the vibrations of the machine which ran almost nonstop. Three babies in diapers!

My husband Larry and I would sleep in the living room on a pull out couch at least until the phone in the kitchen would ring signaling a medical call and a mad scramble to get to it before it woke one of the babies.

I was on overload. My husband was working at Kings County hospital as an intern. To say 24/7 might be an exaggeration, but not by very much.

My mother was my savior. I was tired, bone tired all the time. When she would come it was wonderful. We worked and laughed together. She became my friend. She lifted my spirits. She saved my life. She was marvelous, because she never had a drink in our apartment. How hard that must have been. The trip to and from Flatbush was strenuous. She had bad feet. She once confessed to my sister that one day going home from Flatbush she actually took off her shoes and walked in her stocking feet on the pavement from the bus. You would have to have known my mother to understand the desperation of that gesture.

One day after Larry had been enlisted in a special Air Force program that allowed him to stay in Cornell Medical and then at King's County for internship and we were receiving a pay check each month, we bought a new black Ford sedan.

I had just gotten my license. One of the doctors at Cornell took care of our babies, no charge, so even though we were living in Flatbush I was going to take the babies, Larry and Kevin, to see him at New York Hospital.

The day after we picked up the new car was our first appointment. I figured the route from Brooklyn would not be too bad since I could take the Battery Tunnel and go right onto the FDR and up to 70th Street. Simple! Mom agreed to come out and go with me to help.

I had never driven in a tunnel before and the Brooklyn Battery seemed to me to be far too narrow for my car to fit beside those trucks.

In those days there were Bridge and Tunnel Police patrolling the catwalks in the tunnel and, of course, each one I passed was furiously waving me on. I think I was going pretty slowly. And then I realized, really realized what that phrase, "the light at the end of the tunnel" meant. What a relief to see that little circle of light! As I approached that light the car seemed to not be responding. I couldn't figure out what was the matter. I stepped on the gas but no reaction and as I approached the ramp up out of the tunnel the car slowed and then stopped and started to roll backwards.

My mother was a believer, but didn't make a big show of it. But in an emergency she would start to pray -not loud but in an audible voice, "Jesus, Mary, and Joseph!" "Jesus, Mary and Joseph!" Over and over again. A big, burly cop came over and started yelling at me to get that car out of there. The cars were screeching around us as they exited the tunnel. I told him I couldn't start it.

"Get out!" He said. Disdain does not describe his attitude. He got in and then Little Larry in the baby seat in the front started to scream, really loud. The cop couldn't start it either and finally had to call several guys over to push us out of the way. A friendly officer asked for a hair pin which, of course, my mother had. He fixed the flopper on the carburetor and told me to go right home and go back to the dealer ASAP. When we did, the dealer told us that all those new Fords had the same problem.

"Jesus, Mary and Joseph" was the cry my mother uttered much louder the day years earlier when my brother, Edward, came home from the school-yard with blood apparently pouring out of his eye. As she screamed at me to go get the holy water, Edward kept quietly saying, "Mom, it's alright. I can see you," but the holy water was splashed into his eye and the miracle happened. He could see.

Larry, now Doctor Larry, Doctor Captain Larry, finished his internship at King's County Hospital in Brooklyn and we received his orders: Clark Air force Base in the Philippine Islands. That Labor Day weekend we flew out of Idlewild nonstop to California, on our way to Travis. Three babies, the oldest was two and one half, Kevin was one and one half and Steven was one half, all in diapers. How I wished my mother was with us.

We returned from the P.I. two years later strangely on the same weekend in 1960.

Shortly after our return Mom invited us all for Sunday dinner; a kind of celebration to mark our safe return from the Orient and the fact that we had another new baby, John. By then, Mom and Dad were living at 928 80th Street in the upstairs apartment and Aunt Kay and Uncle Bill in the ground floor. When we got there she was stag-gering drunk. I remember, in front of everyone, and against all my training, I screamed at her for the first and only time in my life; I was furious; I packed up the children and went home.

And home was a bungalow in Rockaway Point. Larry had two months leave in between assignments and it was September so the house in Rockaway, my sister, Joan's really brilliant idea, was perfect. We were too many to stay with either grandmother and Rockaway was about halfway between Bay Ridge and Woodhaven. And it was cheap.

In spite of my outburst, which we never talked about, Mom came down to the beach house often to help. And when she did she was sober. During the last dreary weeks of October when Larry had gone to Georgia to arrange housing and Rockaway was deserted, and while I claimed not to be afraid, she was afraid for me and came and her presence was so welcome. City folk don't like deserted places. Mom was a city person. She wouldn't leave me alone there. The place was particularly sad since there had been a hurricane and lots of the houses were blown away or destroyed. It was a sad place.

And then almost a year later, 1961, when we returned from Georgia, we moved to our first house in Smithtown where Larry was going to start in practice with another doctor. I will never forget my mom's reaction when she saw the house: four bedrooms, two and a half baths, a playroom for the boys right off the kitchen, on half an acre of woods. Truly she thought it was a mansion. So did we. And while the drive from Brooklyn was long, they came often and always in their old, not quite jalopy, of a car. Mom was a Depression baby. She would rather have the money in the bank than indulge her desire to ride comfortably and the thought of borrowing the money was so foreign to her she would not even consider it.

One hot and sultry day in August, Mom and Dad were out visiting. She sensed an oncoming electrical storm and taking Margie, a toddler at the time, by the hand, she went to the end of our driveway calling for the boys to come home from down the street. I was in the kitchen at the sink when I heard the explosion. A ball of lightning had come rolling down the street. She claimed it raised the hairs on her arms, and then it hit the next door neighbor's house putting a hole right through the side of the upstairs bedroom throwing shattered shingles onto our driveway at Mom's feet. Although I couldn't hear her from my kitchen, I feel sure that her prayer," Jesus, Mary and Joseph!" was on her lips.

After the excitement died down and she knew the boys and Maryann and Margie and the neighbor's daughter who had just gotten up from the bed adjoining that wall, were all safe, she said to me in a rather quiet, ominous tone, "Mary, tomorrow we are going to buy a NEW car. Can Larry go with us to help?" And so they did and no car ever gave two people such pleasure, a beautiful burgundy two toned Oldsmobile.

When we added onto the house as the family grew we had a small extra room put in upstairs that was for Mom and Dad so that they would not have to feel that they were putting anyone out when they arrived and I didn't feel that having them sleep on a pull out in the playroom was fair although there were no complaints from them.

Mom and Dad were visiting the weekend of a big anti-war march in Washington. After many meetings locally, I felt it was time for me to put up or shut up and when I asked Mom if she would babysit, she made one condition. She never made conditions, but this time she did and the condition was that I not tell my father where I was going, alone, since Larry was working. Not that Larry's going would have mattered to my father since he always hated any kind of parade or march. They were dangerous and he was against them all, including the St. Pattie's Day Parade in New York City and so if he ever suspected that I was going to Washington D.C. for a demonstration he would have probably physically restrained me.

I don't remember the year, but my mom had a recurring cough that didn't go away. She claimed that she had gone to the doctor in Brooklyn and he was not concerned, but Larry was and finally convinced her to see the ENT doctor in Smithtown, Dr. Haymes. I went with her and remember the doctor coming out to the waiting room and telling me that she had a tumor on her larynx that was very large. He started her on radiation and it seemed to shrink. She was faithful in her visits to him and life went on.

And then I decided to go to law school. I don't remember any conversations with my mother about this life changing event. But I know that she was there, coming out from Brooklyn, staying for a couple of days and then we bought a house in St. James and she, Dad, Aunt Kay and Uncle Bill moved in in January of 1977. In April she suffered a recurrence of the cancer. The doctor in Smithtown referred her to New York City since she had already had radiation locally and they wouldn't do any more at the site.

That June I graduated from St. John's Law School, and was to take the New York State Bar Exam. It was scheduled for two days early in July. We arranged to take my mom into the city for her appointment with the specialist the day before.

It was a Monday. We had to first see the ENT doctor who had offices on Park Avenue and turned out in all respects to be a "Park Avenue" Doctor. He was arrogant. He had four residents in his office all of whom he directed to stick their fingers in my mother's throat so that they could learn what this tumor felt like. Larry was with us and he said to the doctor, "Stop it!" The doctor was not used to anyone telling him anything.

"What do you mean? Why are you here?"

"We had to see you in order to get into Columbia Presbyterian Radiology," Larry said.

"When do you want to go?"

"Today will be fine." I was so proud of him.

And so we did that very afternoon. We had two cars since we were staying overnight in the city so that I should not be late for the Bar Exam the next day and Dad would drive his car home to St. James with my mom.

The doctor at Columbia in the sub-sub-basement of the hospital was everything that the "Park Avenue Doctor" was not. He was gentle and kind and assured my mother that the return of this cancer was not good, but they would try to give her treatment, further radiation five days a week. The appointments were arranged and as we got back up to the street outside it was raining and it was five o'clock and we had had a very hard day.

I didn't want my Dad to get onto the road in all that traffic at that hour. We realized that my brother, the Brother, lived a short distance away from Columbia on Webster Avenue and 165th street in the South Bronx so we quickly arranged to have Larry drive our car and I would take Mom and Dad in Dad's car and we would go to Brother Ed's for dinner. I called from a phone on the street and told his house mates we were coming. He was not home.

Quickly, I got to Ed's house and found his confreres and volunteers there, but he was not home yet. We sat around in the sitting room and to say the conversation was strained is truly an understatement. My poor mother tried her best to make small talk with these total strangers and I kept looking at the clock wondering frantically where my Larry could be. The South Bronx in those days was truly a nightmare place. No phones anywhere, and if one could be found, it didn't work. My mother's eyes told the story. Although she was not saying her prayer audibly, I knew she was working on "Jesus, Mary and Joseph" furiously.

There are events in life that put things into perspective. The Bar Exam was no longer important. My mother's day, and my missing husband, they were really important. It was getting late. Soon it would be dark. Finding Larry became paramount. Brother Ed finally walked in and quickly realized that I had to go look for him. Where? How? Who knew? But I had to look. So Ed said, "Let's go." And as we drove out of his driveway there was Larry driving in. Miracles do really happen.

What I didn't realize was that the last time Larry had been to the South Bronx, the Third Avenue El was still up and he was frantically searching for it. He didn't have any way to contact us and if he did he didn't have Ed's number.

And so the next day I took the New York State Bar Exam, a two day affair, at Lincoln Center Fordham. My Larry went with me to the school and then spent the morning wandering around the city and buying lunch for us and for four or five other as yet unknowns. I found classmates and they were delighted to share lunch. The only condition was that no one speak a word about any part of the dreaded test.

I passed. I soon obtained a job with the Suffolk County District Attorney's Office as an Assistant District Attorney to start that September.

That summer Joan and I took turns taking my Mom into Columbia for radiation five days each week. The Cross Bronx Expressway, previously a terrifying prospect, became a "piece of cake" The treatments were pretty painless except for a skin burning, but she was failing. Eating was difficult. Aunt Kay, living upstairs, would make soft puddings in the hope that she could swallow them. My father took care of her as lovingly as anyone could. My Larry would stop in several times a week. Of course, I would go and visit. She would always be dressed sitting in her chair with an afghan around her knees.

One day in January, 16 months after the diagnosis, she asked me and my sister, Joan, to give her a bed bath since she had not been up to taking a shower for a few days. That night as we undressed and bathed her we realized what the clothes and blanket had hidden. She was so emaciated. We were shocked, but gently we bathed her trying to make small talk to ease her obvious embarrassment. We dressed her in a nice fresh clean nightgown and changed the sheets and finally covered her up and said, "good night".

Joan and I went out to the kitchen with Aunt Kay and had a drink together. We were so shocked at Mom's condition. We didn't realize how bad she was. Larry went in and looked at her and came out of the bedroom and said, "Your mother is dying. You might want to call your brother."

"No, no, she can't be!" I said. But she was. We called Brother Ed. She passed into a calm sleep; I suppose a kind of coma. By midnight, Larry wanted me and my sister to go home assuring us that he was wrong and that she would last a little longer. So Joan and I went home and my brother and father sat by her bedside and at six the next morning, January 18, 1979, my mother died. It was a good death and a good life. She was "my rock and my salvation!" And that is my mother's story.

Memories of My Mother (1944) – clockwise from far left -
Mary, Alice Phelan, Joan, Edward and Edward L.

Mom Reprise

IT HAD BEEN A LONG WEEK: NEW SIDING, NEW WINDOWS REQUIRING WASHED DRAPES, NEW BLINDS — STUFF THAT IS EVENTUALLY REQUIRED IN A FIFTY YEAR OLD HOUSE. So on that Sunday afternoon, after church and the obligatory Sunday brunch at the local diner, it was time to crash. The pile of Sunday papers and the books due to be read all sat waiting beside me on the coffee table that separates my chair from Larry's chair.

That afternoon I quickly succumbed to a nap. I don't dream. I never dream. Although I am frequently told by friends and colleagues that is not true, but rather that I don't remember my dreams. The Jungians claim that all normal folks dream and that it is their unconscious at work. Well maybe my unconscious has been sleeping all these years. All I know is that the last dream I had was when I was about ten years old and I was falling down our cellar stairs, waking just before hitting bottom; a good one for the Jungians to ponder.

But that afternoon as I slept, I looked over at Larry's chair and there was my mother, sitting there large as life. She was smiling at me almost mischievously. I thought, you are not supposed to be here. It was such a good surprise to see her. I hadn't seen her in a long time. She was dressed in her normal clean and starched house dress and in her former healthy state. She had died in 1979 many years after her battle with cancer of the larynx which left her very thin and starved. But there she sat. How to describe her? I think the best word would be contented. She looked over at me and smiled, but did not speak. I can't recall if I spoke to her, but I certainly was pleasantly surprised. Did I say, "What are you doing here?" or did I just think it? I don't know.

But I do know that it was a lovely visitation. I think of my mother very often. I talk to her. I try to tell her that I am so proud of her for the way she overcame her addiction to alcohol. She was a strong undemonstrative lady who was always there when you needed her, no matter how inconvenient it might have been; no matter how hard.

She came and stayed over when I had babies; she came when I had operations; she came when I wanted to take the single day in the city to recover my sanity when the kids were little; she came when I wanted to go to Washington to demonstrate; she came when we dared to go away for a week and then for two weeks' vacation; and she came when I went to law school. She was the mother of three - two little girls who wouldn't dream of misbehaving and a little boy who also didn't get into mischief. When she came to Dogwood Drive she was in charge of a terrible tribe of five boys and two little girls. Not easy for a top sergeant, but really hard for my mom.

I remember the night before she died.

I think about that night and wonder why I never thought of anything that I wanted to say to her, last words and all that. But our relationship was not that kind. And I don't regret it at all since I have open and easy talks with her very often ever since.

Thanks Mom for stopping by.

EDWARD L. - 1928

My Father, Edward L.

PREFATORY AND HISTORICAL NOTE: MY FATHER WAS A GREAT STORYTELLER. His stories were always funny and he told them with relish. He always told us that his older sister, Nellie was the one that brought him up after his mother and then his father died, leaving six young children.

While we were growing up Nellie lived three blocks away from us in Brooklyn. Our address was 672 71st Street, and she lived at 532 Ovington Avenue. She was a single lady as long as I and my sister knew her, working as a ticket agent for the New York BMT Subway at the 95th Street Station which was the end of the Fourth Avenue Line.

Family lore had it that she had been in the Fourteenth Street Station booth when the Sacco and Vanzetti bombing took place and that the bomb blew her socks and shoes clear across the platform. In a sick way we children thought this was a funny story. It needs verification, but for now I do know that my father told us about this and that Nellie was badly injured from the blast, suffering terrible headaches for almost a year during which she was hospitalized in a sanatorium upstate.

Further, Dad told us that Nellie had married a Fopiano before the First World War and that she had a baby. He told of remembering her running down the street toward the hospital with the baby in her arms and screaming for help. The baby died. Fopiano returned from the war having been nerve gassed and become a walking casualty. Further details about him and when he died are unknown.

This all explains Nellie, in a way. She was a kind of semi-recluse. Dad would visit her faithfully and bring us kids. Mom would equally faithfully invite her for Sunday dinner which she would mostly refuse although as I review the older pictures I realize that Nellie is in a lot of them. My recollection that she didn't come so often must be from the later days. Her apartment was comfortable and clean. She visited the hairdresser once every two weeks maintaining her auburn hair color in a neat short cut. Every Christmas after she did not come for dinner Dad would take Joan and I to Nellie's and she would always have one present for each of us. We loved how that extended Christmas.

As Nellie got older and retired from the NY Transit Authority, the only real change was that Dad would visit more often and during the week instead of only on weekends. Eventually Nellie got sick. She would not go to a hospital and Dad did what he could in nursing her. He was with her when she died.

A few days after the funeral, Dad brought home a box of papers from Nellie's apartment. He had cleaned the apartment out and when he came home he put that box up in the closet and in spite of Mom's imprecations to go through the contents, he refused. My father didn't often refuse my mom, but in this instance he refused and didn't want her to go through it either. I believe that he had had so much sadness in his early life that he chose to tell only the funny stories and he knew that the contents of "the box" were all about the sad part of his life and so he simply did not look at it.

And now these many years later I am trying to go through the contents of "the box" which were moved from Eightieth Street and taken to St. James when Mom and Dad and Aunt Kay and Uncle Bill moved out to St. James. The contents of the box got mixed in with other pictures and documents and so now I am trying to write it all down noting what is documented and what is family lore and stories so that you, his progeny can know this wonderful man a little better, a man so full of fun and joy who loved the simple things in life and who was so, so proud of his children and his grandchildren.

My mother eventually, no doubt without Dad's permission, went through that "box" and so there are some papers in my mother's handwriting that show that she tried to write down some of the important facts as she knew them to be.

My Father, Edward Lawrence Phelan, was born in New York City on the 20th of September, 1901, of Mary Holly and Edwin or Edward Phelan.

His mother, Mary Holly Phelan, died at Bellevue Hospital on June 9th, 1906, at 11:33 a.m. having been in hospital from June 5th, 1906, until her death from an "extra uterine pregnancy". This is all documented on her original death certificate which states her age to be 38 years old. Her father was John Holly born in Ireland and her mother was Mary McElligot, also born in Ireland. It doesn't state the counties. The death certificate records that Mary Holly had been in the United States for 19 years, in New York City and that her current residence was 509 Hudson Street and her former residence was 72 Greenwich Street.

There were six children left when Mary Holly Phelan died. They were in order of age: Alice, Helen (Nellie), Mary (Mamie), John (Jackie), my father, Edward and Margaret. All but my father are buried in Calvary Cemetery.

My father's father, Edwin died in 1912 when my father was not yet 11. Dad was thereafter brought up by his older sisters who managed to keep the family together by moving frequently in what was a successful attempt to keep "the Aunts" at bay since they, the children, were convinced that the Aunts planned to place them all in an orphanage. Whether this was in fact true, they believed it and so all contact with aunts and cousins was ended.

On June 24, 1907, my father's father completed payment for a headstone at Calvary that he had had erected in memory of his wife. The cost was $190.00. We have the receipt.

When my brother, Edward, became a De La Salle Christian Brother my father either received or found or wrote a poem on a small card which reads as follows:

I'm the Dad of a Christian Brother

Lord my boy has just been vested
And my joy I cannot hide;
For I've watched him from his childhood
With a father's honest pride.

But the day he left me early
I was feeling mighty blue
Just thinkin' how I'd miss him
And the things we used to do.

But now it's all quite different
Somehow, some way or other
For my heart is ever singing
I'm the Dad of a Christian Brother.

Since to err is only human
There is much upon the slate
That I'll have to take account for
When I reach the Golden Gate.

But then I'm not a worryin'
For I'm a friend of the Blessed Mother
And I'll whisper to Saint Peter
"I'm the Dad of a Christian Brother"

On the back of this card is a hand drawn picture of the funeral monument and in my father's hand is written, "Erected by E. Phelan in memory of his beloved wife Mary E. Phelan nee Holley."(Sp) It is written further," On the bottom of stone the name PHELAN" This is in parenthesis and then it reads in Poppa's hand,
"New Inscriptions
1868- Mary E. Phelan -1906
1863- Ed. Phelan -1912
1890- Alice E. Hansen-1947
1895- Mary Manzo-1968
1904- Margaret Lynch- 1968

"Calvary Semitary"(sp) Sec 33 Range 1- Plot C. Grave 27&28 St. Elizabeth Ave 8 graves in from sign sec. 33- opposite sign sec 32 right turn after ses.#22 sharp left at end of street- to middle of next st. on right side."

Nellie was not on this writing since she was still alive. According to her death certificate she died on June 19, 1972, having been born on August 26, 1893, which made her the second oldest, but family lore had it that the oldest, Alice was not so much involved in the bringing up of the younger ones in the family. Nellie's death certificate shows that she was widowed having been married to a Fopiano, that she had been a ticket agent (retired) and that she was buried at Calvary Cemetery. By then we had moved to 80th Street, Brooklyn, shortly before the old neighborhood gave way to the cut through for the new Verrazano Bridge.

There was a saying in the old days that sometimes someone was "no good". What that phrase meant exactly was never explained but it implied all sorts of things none of which were good. My father's sister, Alice, was so described and she died, at King's Park Psychiatric Center on November, 8, 1947.

My mother told me that Dad used to go out there by LIRR to visit her once a month until she died. I have no knowledge how or when or why she was there but I know from personal experience that it was a terrible place. Her name at her death was Alice Veronica Hansen and Nellie paid $305.15 for her funeral expenses. But there is a business card in the papers from "the box" for an

Edward J. Taylor, Contractor with an address of 3954 Janett Ave. Cincinnati, Ohio, 45211, on the back of which in my Mother's handwriting is the following:

"Edw J Taylor is the son of Alice Taylor sister of Edward L Phelan also Helen Mary Margaret John"

The only other remnant of Alice in the papers is an envelope on which is written "In Memory of my Mother Deceased June 9th, 1906, signed Alice" Inside is an older envelope with the same inscription. It contains a lock of bright red hair and a cloth scapular-like piece with a crown suspended over what appears to be the letter M and a piece of bright green ribbon which may have tied the lock of hair at one time.

There is also a receipt for $5.00 for "Blessing at Calvary Chapel Friday 2:40 p.m. Oct. 24, 1947 Alice Hansen" Since Alice was born in 1890 she must have been just sixteen years old at the time of her mother's death with five siblings ranging in age from two to thirteen. Somehow as the oldest she managed to keep the family together at least for those early years.

Dad used to tell the story that he remembered when both Alice and Nellie, went to work and would come home on Friday with a little money and send him out to get an ice cream soda and how he would get it in a tin beer bucket and would reach in on his way home and scoop the ball of strawberry ice cream out and lick it since he was sure they wouldn't give him much once he got home.

There is also what appears to be an old newspaper obituary for Elizabeth (nee Holly) O'Connor which reads as follows:

"August 26th, beloved mother of Helen and Nora. Native of Balingoun, County Kerry. Funeral from her home, 35 W. 89th St. Solemn Requiem Mass St. Gregory's Church, 144 W. 90th St., Monday 10a.m. Internment Calvary."

We can only assume that this was a sister of Mary Holly Phelan and an aunt to the six children.

There are further notes in my Mother's hand, printed notes that show Mary Manzo Nov 30, 1895-1968 and Margaret Lynch April 19, 1904- April 1, 1968 with the age 64 circled.

Margaret was Poppa's younger sister who I remember seeing at Aunt Nellie's on occasion. She was very pretty but her husband was short and not very good looking. He was a twin, a fact which Joan and I found very strange and amusing. We didn't know any twins at that time.

How strange it is to think that the fact of twinning has become so common and one wonders whether it is the effect of improved pre-natal care or of some other anomaly. Margaret worked for Higgins Ink which manufactured ink in all colors and so we occasionally had a present of a box of colored inks but our mother didn't really appreciate such a gift since the ink was indelible.

In later years, when we moved to Smithtown, there was an old stone house on Edgewood and Landing Avenues that my Dad used to say was previously owned by the owner of Higgins Ink and some comments of his or of my Mother's gave rise to certain nuances, the details of which I can no longer remember, but they gave my grownup-self reason to think that there had been some relationship between Margaret and the fellow who owned the company beyond that of employer/employee.

We have Dad's original working papers which were issued to him on Sept 29, 1915, in which he is described as 5 feet, 84 lbs., living at 90 Baltic Street with gray eyes. It is signed by Edward L. Phalen. Is it that his spelling was poor or that the name was supposed to be spelled that way? Or was it that the nuns in school spelled it wrong and there was no mom or dad to correct them? What is even stranger is that my Father always said that he was a redhead even when there was no semblance of red in his hair and he had the bluest eyes of anyone.

But all this doesn't really describe my father, Edward L. That's how he signed all of his cards to his children, his grandchildren and anyone else to whom he might be writing. He was the happiest person in the world; he didn't care about things. Well there was that one thing he cared about - that new car; he took care of that Oldsmobile as though it were a new baby. He took it back and forth to the Old's Dealer for every assigned checkup, over my husband's protestations that the dealer was so much more expensive than the local mechanic.

He was fun, he was funny, he was a 'modern man' long before that term was even thought of. After a big dinner in our dining room, before anyone thought of cleaning up, he would be in the kitchen doing dishes and in the midst of the job he would put the dish towel over his head babushka style and peek into the dining room and make some remark that led to gales of laughter.

He was a rabble rouser. He loved a good argument. He was so proud of the fact that the New York Post labeled him a "red", a "Commie" for his efforts in trying to form the NYC PBA. He went from precinct to precinct trying to rouse the men to understand the need for organization. They would bang the chair seats to drown out his message. Eventually, he became the Recording Secretary of that fledgling organization.

In short, my father was a loving, gentle, fun and funny man.

Poppa, Kay and Ed - 1977

Remembrance of Aunt Kay

Aunt Kay, Catherine Powers, was born on July 7th, 1907, and she died on March 26th, 2003.

On that Friday night at the funeral home my mind was so full and so weary, I could not speak the words I truly felt. But I had to commit my thoughts - scattered and jumbled though they were - to paper lest we forget that the Aunt Kay in the box whom we didn't even recognize and the Katie from the Nursing Home who was such an uncomplaining patient, were not the Aunt Kay I will always remember.

My first memories are from 71st Street in Brooklyn where on a weekday evening; Aunt Kay would come after dinner and Uncle Bill would drive her. She had a driver's license which she faithfully renewed every year, but no one ever saw her drive. She never came empty handed - always some little something for Joan and me from the 5 and 10 cent store. Sometimes now I think perhaps it was unfair to our mom who couldn't or wouldn't do those things. But Gaga never expressed by word or intimation her disapproval if such there was.

Katie always felt cold and I can see her in our kitchen arms folded, leaning against the radiator to warm up. Many times, always special, we stayed overnight at our Nana's in Senator Street. Joan and I would sleep in Aunt Kay's bed with her. I remember how spooked Joan and I used to be staring at that picture of Our Lady of Perpetual Help which hung at the end of her bed. Its eyes would follow you wherever you were in the room. Joan would go to the window and I to the door, but her eyes followed us both. I still have that picture and it still scares me.

In the bottom drawer of the bureau in that bedroom were Aunt Kay's old high heel shoes and old hats which she saved for us. Joan and I had many long hours of great make believe and dress up fun from that one drawer.

Then there were the happy, happy summers we spent in the Highlands, Joan and I and Nana; and Aunt Kay and Uncle Bill on the weekends.

Life galloped along and Aunt Kay was always there. I remember our first Christmas in Smithtown. We were looking forward to getting together with my sister's family (the McCormack cousins) in New Hyde Park after having spent two years in the Philippines and one in Albany, Georgia. By Christmas Eve, Kevin, Steven and John broke out with chicken pox and the real live tree that we bought as new home owners always do bled brown muddy stuff all over the living room carpet by Christmas morning and a big snow storm blew in overnight. Suddenly, in spite of the snow, there were Kay and Bill pulling into the driveway loaded with gifts and good cheer. She was that way, not a big talker just a doer, someone who took care of everybody.

She and my mother took care of their father, John Powers, a big man, who suffered several strokes and was a handful for Nana who never broke 100 pounds or five feet. Sometimes he would fall out of bed and if Nana were alone she would ask the garbage men to come upstairs and help her get him up off the floor. What is really strange from our present perspective is that they would do it. She would give them a 'little something'.

After John Powers, our grandfather, died Katie took care of Nana, Bridget Daly Powers, cooking supper every night for her and Bill after she came home from work.. Some days she would be peeling the potatoes before she even took her coat off.

And then mom got sick, cancer of the larynx and by then Kay and Bill had moved to Eightieth Street with Mom and Dad. Gaga miraculously got better and I went to Law School and in December 1976 we bought the house in St. James for them.

Mom was getting herself into a terrible anxious state worrying about how she was going to make the move, go through all the stuff, etc. and so my brother, Edward, and I decided against the strong advice of Joan, to move them surreptitiously. I invited them all out for one of the kid's Christmas concerts. Meanwhile, Edward and all of the remaining male and female kids, with a hired truck and a borrowed one moved everything from 80th street to St. James; that was two fully furnished floors, and a rather full basement!

There were some wild stories about the back door of one of the vans opening and stuff falling out on the Belt Parkway that I am thankfully not privy to.

After the concert, we decided to stop in St. James to show the house to Aunt Kay and Uncle Bill - Mom had seen it many times - and surprise them all with the move. Low and behold when they walked in everything was set in place; furniture in place, pictures and the big mirror hung, dishes in the closets. After looking like they were going to die or pass out, there came a look in their eyes, the four of them, a look of relief, a kind of sigh, "It's done, we don't have to worry about it", and while 26 years have given me more Joan's view of this caper, Aunt Kay and Mom never really yelled at us or even looked upset. The furniture stayed just where it had been put that day.

And every day, Kay and Bill and Mom and Dad, as long as they were able went to daily Mass and when Mom got sick shortly after the move Aunt

Kay would make her soup and puddings and soft stuff to help her eat.

And she was there the day Mom died.

And then Kay took care of Uncle Bill. When Bill died Katie moved downstairs and took care of Dad. Then on a beautiful, sunny Sunday morning in September 1983, we all went to Mass together, Dad, Aunt Kay, Larry and I and many of the kids. At breakfast at Friendly's the kids pumped Dad, whom they all called Poppa, to retell his favorite stories and we all laughed; the guy who fell down the elevator shaft; the piano crashing as Dad in his youth and his friends tried to lower it down from the top floor of a tenement in Brooklyn, with ropes and tackle and the chimney giving way and the piano crashing to the sidewalk and Dad and his friends disappearing; the horse with the sore on its back. He had a way of making really serious stories very funny. It was a particularly uproarious occasion and after fighting as usual over the check, I took them home to St. James. Not long after Aunt Kay called to say that something was wrong with Dad. He had gone outside to sit in his favorite chair in the sunny porch, put his head back and died.

Katie was alone. How terrifying it must have been for her and yet she never did give voice to her fears, always "I'm fine." Little Larry moved in upstairs with his first wife, Maria, but she was not much company for Kay. Subsequently, Margie and her husband Paul moved in and were great company for her, but when they moved out Katie moved in with us and eventually after many falls and some close calls with the stove she went into the nursing home. At first she had a roommate, Sarah, and things were pretty good. But then she fell, broke her wrist and couldn't use the walker and then couldn't walk and it was downhill from there. But through it all, no complaints.

She worked for Kendall Mills as an executive secretary all of fifty years. Every baby in the family had the benefit of diapers she would get after the season. Samples; we had elephants and donkeys during election years, and rosebuds and daffodils at Easter and flags at the Fourth of July and Christmas Wreaths in season. Memories also include manual typewriters, fans not air conditioners, girdles and stockings and one hour off early when the temperature broke ninety and never a hair out of place and always she was dressed to the nines.

Thanks for everything, Aunt Kay and Happy Birthday!

THE GANG IN 1966 – FROM L. TO R. BILL POWERS, KAY POWERS,
NELLIE PHELAN, EDWARD L. AND ALICE POWERS PHELAN

LARRY WERNER - 2010

Number Ten

MY HUSBAND, LARRY WERNER, DOCTOR LARRY WERNER, DIED ON JULY 19TH, THIS YEAR, 2012, SUDDENLY. He really died on the 17th in my arms at his doctor's office where we went for a cough that was bothering him. Of course, all the efforts of that doctor and the ambulance crew for resuscitation actually worked and so for the next couple of days in the hospital his body breathed, his blood pressure normal, his heartbeat remained normal. But I knew he was dead and the EEG conducted on the next morning confirmed that. Life support was withdrawn, but his body continued. They said something about the brain stem continuing to work.

It was strange, but good. Our family had time to come and to say their last words and to sit and hold his hand. Fortunately, while he was actually dead his countenance was normal; a little smile seemed to be there. It was comforting for them. And then two days later officially he was pronounced dead.

But those two days were really good. We had time to visit the funeral home, to spend some precious hours to arrange his funeral liturgy, a very personal expression of his wonderful life. Every one of our children and grandchildren participated. Maryann did the music. Her daughter an accomplished flutist and her son, a talented euphonium player and music major composed the music. They played before the service began and after Communion. It was beautiful.

Each of the grandchildren read a petition that reflected the various aspects of Larry's life: his great love for them and for me; his life as a healer, as a prophet, as a lover of the cosmic world and the earth; his efforts to convert "either/or" thinking to "both/and"; his love of learning; his grace in aging and especially his ability to focus on the moment.

The service in the Catholic Liturgy of Christian Burial begins by the placement of a large white pall on the coffin before it enters the church, intended to remind us of baptism and the completion of that baptism at death. I insisted that since I was sure most did not know of that particular symbolism, I wanted to place our family baptism dress on the coffin as well and I did.

I had for a long time talked about this to my children so that they would know where the dress was and that it was washed and starched and pressed and ready for whomever would need it first. They didn't want to talk about it. Death is hard even when it hasn't occurred yet.

The service was beautiful. Our sons Steven and Paul did the readings. Margaret read the Psalm. Actually, she was the first to volunteer. My brother Edward read the Gospel. Our five sons brought the gifts to the Offertory. And all the children carried their father into and out of the Church.

The wake for the previous day and a half had been a wonderful, difficult parade of all the friends old and new, the former patients, the acquaintances, the people whose lives he had touched. And then the burial. Done. Death. Done.

The next three weeks I spent writing thank you notes for all the Prayer Cards and Masses, the flowers, the food. And all the while our family made sure I was not alone. In between I would go out on the deck and sit quietly, resting my arm and hand and smoking for the first time in years while talking to him and to God. In some way Larry was present.

He is still present. I don't mean in some spooky way, but rather in a real sense. He told me I didn't have to do that, the cards that is, but I did, for me. And then as the family returned to their respective homes near and far, I started to do the closet, to pack all of his clothes in boxes for Big Brothers Big Sisters. It was easier than I thought it would be.

Today I got to his dresser top drawers. There were all the normal things, screws and odd nuts and bolts, and match books and change but then

I found the notes, written on prescription paper, from his Landing Avenue office. The writing was strong with messages from him to me. When he wrote them I don't know. On one was written in his hand, "Here's looking at you, Kid. Remember me?", and on the other, "Emancipation Proc: You are free."

But then there was a little note book, two by four inches, no lines, and with one entry:

1 Working at NY-NJ PA- young kid
2 Mother of 7-
3 Teacher of deaf
4 Student - College
5 Student - Law School
6 Assistant DA
7 Judge
8 Health Aid
9 Redired Lady
10

Each number was circled. The paper was not old. The writing was not strong like the others. He misspelled "red-haired" or did he mean "retired". He left number ten blank.

Clearly he had listed the stages of my life, each one he helped me to achieve and obviously the last had to be "widow". I hate that word. It is a mournful, sad, dreary word; and even worse a mournful, sad, dreary state. I had to find another word, a different word. Words matter. With his list in hand I decided, I would *now* be a NUMBER TEN.

Thank you, my dearest love and constant companion for over 60 wonderful, exciting, adventurous years. I don't understand the question mark, but I will always remember you. I cannot do otherwise. You are here every day in every way.

Love,
NUMBER TEN

FAMILY AT GOSHEN (1995) – FROM L. TO R. KEVIN, MARYANN, LITTLE LARRY MARY, JOHN, BIG LARRY, PAUL, MARGIE AND STEVEN

Afterword

OUR MOTHER HAS BEEN WORKING ON HER MEMOIRS HER ENTIRE LIFE. Of late she has been committing them to paper. We have not yet seen them but nevertheless have long been privileged and privy to the cavalcade that is their content. So it is with no small conceit that we even attempt to add anything since we possess no qualifications for this task other than genetic accident.

Nevertheless, on the occasion of our mother's eightieth birthday we felt it incumbent that we children should try to say something about our mother; and, in so saying, by necessity to also include our father; *qua definitione.* It is not our intention to write this as an elegiac, as we can all attest that our mother is very much alive; and our father lives on through her, in our memories, and in all of us.

We have had the great good fortune to have been raised by and come to know these two most exemplary people; righteous without self-righteousness, nurturing, teachers who never lost the wonder of being students, genuinely humble, they lived their lives able to see the humor in all things, to feel empathy for all suffering, to feel and share others' joy without jealousy; zealously religious without zealotry; deeply faithful to their God, to themselves, to each other, to all of us, and to the world.

They say that you can tell a lot about people by their friends. Our parents have surrounded themselves with an ever-expanding group of equally upstanding and likeable people with whom they have maintained friendships spanning lifetimes and beyond. We all would like to feel that while we will never matriculate from being their children, we have in fact graduated into their circle of friendship.

They never complained about what they might have given up in their devotion to us and then, our families. It is apparent that they never considered it as having given up anything. We, as members of our parents' congregation, feel that their pastorship and spiritual guidance could not be equaled by any member of the clergy. They truly have answered their vocations and fulfilled their vows to themselves, to each other, to us, and to the very world. We all are better for their presence.

They did always and our mother continues to remind us that our voices are important and our rights sacrosanct .Raising seven children with an even temper even when we gave them so little reason to be so and to do so while both being professionals of the very highest caliber speaks volumes of their abilities: indomitable, dignified, modest, indefatigable, never playing favorites....we could never say enough.

We just wanted to take this moment to thank them and especially you Mom for having been and continuing to be a most powerful example. We all hope that we can in some way carry on with your legacy and live it for you, for us, for our children, and for the world as you have and continue to do. We learned about love from the best teachers.

With all our love,
LKSJMPM

MORE FAMILY – MARCH 17, 2012

CHRISTMAS PHOTO - 2000

The Editor

A S ANYONE WHO HAS READ THIS BOOK REALIZES IT IS COMPOSED OF SMALL BITS AND PIECES, MEMOIRS THAT I HAVE WRITTEN OVER THE COURSE OF SIX YEARS AND IN NO WAY CONTAINS THE WHOLE STORY OF MY LIFE. My children decided that for my eightieth birthday they would publish them. Of course, they needed a lot of editing, a lot of work, and probably still do but it is time to stop and say it is done. But I can't say that without crediting my main collaborator and editor, my computer maven, my best critic, my daughter, Maryann Hartwick, trained as a biologist, and now a tax adviser and amateur astronomer. And I can't end without a story about her.

When she was to be confirmed the first step in the religious education program was for the kids to choose a name, a saint's name, and hand it in on a card. The director of Religious Education, then and for many years thereafter, was Mrs. Georgia Priebe, a good friend. When she got Maryann's selection, Holly, she was appalled.

"That's not a saint's name! What's wrong with Mary Werner letting her daughter select such a name?"

But then the second step was for the kids to write a letter explaining their choice of saint's name and Maryann wrote a beautiful letter explaining about her great grandmother, Mary Holly Phelan, and her life and her death and that she was a real saint. Georgia was moved to tears. Here was one kid that really got it!

Thank you Maryann Holly Werner Hartwick for all your help, all your time, all your support, for everything.

Love, Mom

Made in the USA
Lexington, KY
29 July 2013